The Englang Pronunciation Course For Learners of English

An advanced course in pronunciation and intonation designed for the classroom and for self-study

by

Keith Hollingsworth

and

Laura Park

illustrated by Jonathan Marks

ENGLANG BOOKS

SOUTHAMPTON

ENGLANG BOOKS
17 BOND ROAD
SOUTHAMPTON SO18 1LR
ENGLAND

First published 2000
Reprinted with corrections 2003

ISBN 1 871819 60 1 The Englang Pronunciation Course

Also available in this series:

ISBN 1 871819 20 2	German-English False Friends, Book 1
ISBN 1 871819 15 6	German-English False Friends, Book 2
ISBN 1 871819 25 3	German-English False Friends, Book 3
ISBN 1 871819 10 5	101 Myths About The English Language
ISBN 1 871819 35 0	Which Words?
ISBN 1 871819 30 X	Pizazz!
ISBN 1 871819 55 5	Cartoons For Learning English
ISBN 1 871819 50 4	Practice With Prepositions
ISBN 1 871819 45 8	The Mistakes Clinic

Typeset by Englang Books

Printed by Hobbs The Printers of Southampton

Contents

Acknowledgment

Sincere thanks go to Tony Addison, longtime Lecturer in English Phonetics at the University of Göttingen, Germany. He worked painstakingly through many of the trickiest sections of the manuscript, and his comments, corrections and suggestions for improvements have been invaluable. In particular he has given detailed advice on intonation patterns and on the transcription of phrases and sentences. Whilst it should not be assumed that all the final versions given in this book would meet with his approval (pronunciation teachers very rarely agree on everything!), it is certainly true that his ideas have played a significant part in modifying the versions given.

Tape

Throughout the book you will see some sections marked with a cassette symbol:

This symbol indicates two things:

(1) where a dialogue follows, the whole of that dialogue is on the tape;

(2) where example sentences or exercises follow, it is normally **the first two columns** of word lists which can be found on the tape. The remaining columns should, for extra practice, be read aloud in the same manner as the exercises on the tape.

Transcriptions

Most units in the book contain some amusing sentences in phonetic script. These include jokes, sayings, quotations and aphorisms. It is extremely important to bear in mind that the transcriptions of words in sentences is very often quite different from the transcriptions of those same words in isolation or in short phrases. For example, "Who" would always be transcribed /huː/ in isolation, but could be /huː/, /hu/ or /u/ in a sentence, depending on its environment. The transcriptions are intended to indicate the speech of an educated native speaker of Standard Southern British English, talking at normal speed to another native speaker.

It should also be borne in mind - especially with regard to intonation and stress - that there is always more than one way of saying something. The transcription of each sentence is intended to illustrate the intonation / stress pattern which is either the most likely or one of the most likely.

General Introduction

Why do some students achieve better results in pronunciation and intonation than others? Is it only a matter of natural ability? Research has shown that natural ability is **less** important than:

- the mother tongue of the learner (eg. Dutch people tend to find speaking the sounds of English easier than Spanish people);

- the "strength of concern" (i.e. recognition of the importance of pronunciation and intonation);

- contact with native speakers.

Although we cannot change our native language, this is good news for students because it shows that they **can** improve significantly if they believe in the importance of these skills and can take advantage of frequent contact with native speakers.

This course is intended to be a practical aid towards very good speaking skills and specifically targets the typical problems of foreign speakers who have been learning English for several years. The course can be used as a full pronunciation / intonation course in a language laboratory or normal classroom with an instructor; as a supplement to a general language course; or for individual study. The standard of English is high and aimed at universities, colleges and language schools, but linguistic theory is only included as far as it aids the practical application. Unfortunately, pronunciation and intonation skills are sometimes neglected in schools and foreign speakers often need help in establishing where their errors lie, as well as a concentrated learning programme. In some ways it is unfortunate that many native English speakers have developed great tolerance in trying to understand foreigners speaking English and are often unwilling to correct learners because this would seem impolite.

The course does not limit itself to pure pronunciation and intonation alone, but, in an attempt to reflect the interplay of general language skills, also practises the relationship between sounds and spelling (notoriously difficult in this rather non-phonetic language) and offers exercises in general conversation, vocabulary and writing. Finally, it should be stressed that listening is the key to good pronunciation and intonation: you should concentrate on careful listening to native speakers so that you can reproduce their sounds in your own pronunciation and intonation.

Introduction: for teachers

Aims of the course

This course tries to improve the mastering of sounds, stress and intonation, the main elements of speaking. Students themselves are often unaware of their personal mistakes and teachers should point these out gently and tactfully. When it comes to criticism of their speaking ability, students tend to react more sensitively than they do to criticism of their grammar or vocabulary skills. As indicated above the problems of the student largely depend on her / his native language. French or Spanish students, for example, often find it difficult to distinguish between *seat* (/iː/) and *sit* (/ɪ/) whereas Germans would find no difficulty here. The teacher needs, therefore, to select the sections most relevant to the students.

Sounds

A problem sound presents two main stages for the student: firstly, being able to articulate the sound correctly when concentrating on it, and secondly, being able to articulate the sound automatically without specifically concentrating on it. The first stage is usually fairly easy and can be done quickly and effectively in class but the second often means frequent individual practice. Once sounds become automatic, however, they will rarely be pronounced wrongly.

Stress and intonation

Stress and intonation are closely connected and reflect the rhythm and music of the language. Practising word stress is very helpful as the positions of stressed syllables can be complicated. Wrongly stressed syllables can quickly lead to misunderstandings, as in **pho**tograph - pho**to**grapher - photo**graph**ic. Intonation reflects meaning and the melodies of language. Students need to accustom themselves to these melodies just as they would to a pop song. Foreign speakers often simply transfer the melodies of their native tongue to English: they may usually be understood but their English sounds distinctly "foreign". Few students enjoy good intonation skills and those who do have mostly spent an extended period abroad or have worked very hard individually. Intonation patterns in English are complicated, and in our own teaching we have found explanations of linguistic theory to be of limited practical value. We have therefore concentrated on the basics of word stress, sentence stress (highlighting) and a few common patterns. In this way it is hoped that student sensitivity to intonation can be heightened.

Organisation

The course is organised into 13 units with some progression from unit to unit but the teacher could easily select only those sections relevant to the class. Almost every unit deals with a typical pronunciation problem and some aspect of intonation or word stress.

It is assumed that students need to learn to use the phonemic alphabet, firstly so that they become fully aware of how words are really being pronounced and secondly so that they can look up the pronunciation of new words in a learners' dictionary. Moreover, as English spelling is often illogical and unphonetic, some emphasis is placed on the relationship between the spoken and the written word. We have also included a number of assignments which provide both speaking practice (with students' own dialogues) and writing practice. Answers to all of the main exercises can be found in the key at the end of the book, but there are also some exercises where students, instead of turning to the key, are required to consult a good monolingual dictionary to check stress, spelling, etc. Encouraging self-help in this way lies in the best interests of all students.

Introduction: for students

Question: What is the greatest compliment any English native speaker could pay you?

Answer: You're German / French etc.? Oh, I thought you were English!

Impossible? No, not at all. Of course, it depends on the context: the topic of conversation, who you are talking to, the mood you are in, etc. Perhaps you feel your skills are already good because English native speakers understand you and maybe they have complimented you on your good English. You should, of course, enjoy such compliments but the British and Americans are fairly easy to impress (after all, how many can speak a foreign language fluently?), they like to be friendly and don't like to be critical. Trying to get a native speaker to correct you when you make mistakes can be very frustrating!

This coursebook has been designed to help you improve your speaking skills in a practical way. You first need to find out where your problems lie. If you have been saying a sound like the English /r/ wrongly for seven years it can be a time-consuming business to correct it. However, with determination and a few hours of regular weekly practice, it **is** possible to overcome your problems. With such problems there are two stages:

(1) acquiring the ability to articulate the sound correctly when you concentrate on that sound alone;

(2) practising so much that you automatically say it correctly in a sentence and during longer conversations.

The first stage is often fairly easy but the second usually needs time and determination. Most students find intonation especially difficult. This book practises some of the important aspects and should make you more aware of the problems. You can also improve a lot by listening to native speakers (your teacher, host family, radio etc.) and trying to copy the melodies of their speech patterns.

For those working alone

If you are working alone you can either work systematically through the book and cassette, going quickly through the sections you find easy, or you can work on those sections which are most relevant to you. You should find out where your problems lie. What are the typical problems for speakers of your mother tongue? Look at the sounds on the contents page. Which sounds seem more difficult? Listen carefully to the cassette and try to imitate carefully. Try to have some contact with a native speaker, or listen carefully to native speakers on the radio or TV. It is better to practise for 15 - 20 minutes every day than for two or three hours at the weekend.

Notes on American Pronunciation

As some students understandably find it difficult to separate British R.P. (Br.E.) and General American (Am.E.) pronunciations, a list of the **main** differences is included, together with examples:

	Br.E.	**Am.E.**	**Comments**
Vowels			
cot	ɒ	ɑː	Am.E. open and long, rhymes with Br.E. *art*
taught	ɔː	ɑː	Am.E. open, rhymes with Br.E. *tart*
last	ɑː	æ	Am.E. open as in Br.E. *cat*, (although some words as Br.E. e.g. *father*)
near	ɪə	ɪᵊr	Can be a pure vowel in Am.E.
fair	eᵊ	eᵊr	Can be a pure vowel in Am.E.
duty	juː	uː	Am.E. often misses out the /j/ in words where a 'u' follows a 't', 'th' 'd', or 'n', as in *dupe, enthusiasm, new, tune.*
vermin	ɪ	ə	In Am.E., vowel sounds in unstressed syllables are even more often /ə/ than in Br.E. In Am.E. *Herman* and *vermin* rhyme.
missile	aɪl	l	In Am.E., words ending '-ile' typically have a syllabic 'l', e.g. *docile, facile, fertile, sterile, virile.*
anti-	i	aɪ	Typical examples: *anti-authoritarian, anti-Communist, anti-Semitic.*
semi-	i	aɪ	As in *semifinal, semi-professional.*
Consonants			
metal	t	d	Am.E. *metal* sounds like Br.E. *medal.*
car	-	r	The letter 'r' in Am.E is always pronounced.
saw it	intrusive 'sɔːrɪt	r 'sɑː ɪt	In Am.E. no linking is made here:

Elision

Long words ending in '-ery', '-ary', or '-ory' usually have the 'er', 'ar' or 'or' elided in Br.E., but not in Am.E.:

	Br.E.	**Am.E.**
mandatory	'mændətri	'mændə,tɔːri
solitary	'sɒlətri	'sɑːlə,teri
temporary	'tempri	'tempə,reri

Individual words

Some individual words are pronounced differently:

	Br.E.	**Am.E.**
tomato	tə'mɑːtəʊ	tə'meɪtəʊ
clerk	klɑːk	klɜːrk
derby	'dɑːbi	'dɜːrbi
vitamin	'vɪtəmɪn	'vaɪtəmɪn
borough	'bʌrə	'bɜːroʊ
thorough	'θʌrə	'θʌroʊ

Word stress

Am.E. sometimes uses a different stress pattern. This may involve a shift of stress from the second to the first syllable or vice versa. However, it is becoming increasingly common to hear American stress forms in British English. The most important category is two-syllable words of French origin, where Br.E. normally has stress on the first syllable and Am.E. on the second. These are listed under (a) below; others are listed under (b).

		Br.E.	**Am.E.**
(a)	ballet	'bæleɪ	bæ'leɪ
	beret	'bereɪ, 'beri	bə'reɪ
	brochure	'brəʊʃə	broʊ'ʃʊᵊr
	fillet	'fɪlɪt	fɪ'leɪ
	pâté	'pæteɪ	pɑː'teɪ
	purée	'pjʊəreɪ	pjʊ'reɪ
(b)	cigarette	sɪgə'ret	'sɪgəret
	details	'diːteɪlz	dɪ'teɪlz
	magazine	,mægə'ziːn	'mægəziːn

Notes on word stress and intonation patterns

Word Stress

Rules for word stress in English are fairly complicated and the most common patterns are explained and practised in the individual units. However, there are some important points which should be emphasised in this introduction to the topic:

(1) Word stress in polysyllabic words is **variable**, i.e. it can come on completely different syllables for different words, even if those words are of similar length:

certain, per**for**mance, infor**ma**tion, aqua**marine.**

(2) Word stress in English is **mobile**, i.e. it can shift according to grammatical form or the addition of suffixes. These shifts are generally part of common patterns:

(a) In two-syllable words which exist both as verbs and as nouns or adjectives, the rule is:
noun (or adjective) - first-syllable stress; verb - second-syllable stress:

nouns:	an **ex**port	a **re**cord	a **sur**vey	a **sub**ject
verbs:	to ex**port**	to re**cord**	to sur**vey**	to sub**ject**

(b) Adding an '-ic' suffix shifts the stress to the syllable before that suffix:

climate - cli**mat**ic　　**em**phasis - em**phat**ic
drama - dra**mat**ic　　ge**og**raphy - geo**graph**ic

Note, however, that adding an '-able' suffix does ***not*** shift the stress:

knowledge - **know**ledgeable　　re**ly** - re**li**able

(3) In polysyllabic words we can distinguish between three types of word stress:

- primary stress, the main stress, which is marked with a ' :

  primary 'praɪməri　　character 'kærɪktə

- secondary stress, which shows there is no vowel reduction or weak form, and is marked with a ˌ :

  conversation ˌkɒnvə'seɪʃn　　superstition ˌsuːpə'stɪʃn

- tertiary stress, which shows a short pause in a multi-syllable word, and is marked with ̥ :

  intercommunication ˌɪntəkə̥ mjuːnɪ'keɪʃən
  public address system ˌpʌblɪk ə'dres̥ sɪstəm

However, tertiary stress is not included in the units as its helpfulness in pronouncing new words is doubtful. (See p.20 for the stress symbols used in this book.)

(4) A basic feature of the word stress system in English is the use, in unstressed syllables, of so-called "reduced" vowels. These are known as ***weak forms***, and occur most often in the form /ə/ and, less often, as /ɪ/.
Of all vowels in connected spoken English approximately 25% are the /ə/, or "schwa" sound, and 20% the /ɪ/, (making them the most common English vowels by far.) These reduced vowels enable the speaker to speak faster and they are used both in unstressed syllables of polysyllabic words as well as in unstressed monosyllabic words:

person pɜːsən *but* personify pə'sɒnɪfaɪ
I came home from work at two o'clock. frəm ət ə

This is a big problem for most learners of English, who tend to pronounce all vowels in their strong form, thereby giving their pronunciation a definite foreign accent.

Intonation

Intonation is the general name given to the way our voices unconsciously move up and down the scale of pitch in order to reflect and give added meaning to the words we are speaking. This can be compared to body language such as facial expressions and gestures. In other words, meaning is not only expressed through words, but by body language and intonation too. We can best illustrate the role of intonation by pronouncing identical words and phrases with different intonation patterns and thereby changing the meanings. If someone, for example, asked us whether we liked a certain film we had just seen, our answer, "Yes", could be expressed with a variety of intonations, depending on our intended meaning:

(I liked the film but I don't want to talk about it.)

(I loved the film - it was great!)

(I partly liked the film, but I have some reservations.)

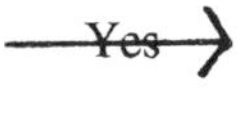

(I thought the film was boring.)

Here we can see that intonation creates meaning and should not be ignored by learners. As intonation is the raising and lowering of the voice on the stressed and unstressed syllables, it is closely interconnected with word stress. In order to demonstrate the elements and functions of intonation we have written a short dialogue set in a clothes shop. Listen carefully to the dialogue and use this as a basis for understanding the following sections on intonation:

Joan: *Eamonn, come and look at this. I rather like this pullover.*

Eamonn: *It's very nice. But Joan, will it fit you?*

Joan: *Hmm, maybe it's a bit small. What about that red one?*

Eamonn: *Yes, but the material's synthetic, isn't it?*

Joan: *Yes, you're right. What do you think of this bright yellow one?*

Eamonn: *Oh no, it's awful! You're not serious, are you? Don't buy that one! The people who wear yellow are old-fashioned.*

Joan: *I suppose so. We'll go home now, O.K.? Come on then. By the way, whose favourite colour is yellow?*

Elements of intonation

tone group This is a unit of language whose words are naturally spoken together and has one, possibly two, prominent syllables which highlight significant words. The boundaries of tone groups are indicated with parallel slashes and the prominent syllables are written here in bold.

> **Ea**monn |, **come** and look at **this**. | I **ra**ther like this **pull**over.

tonic This is the most prominent syllable in the tone group and one which carries a pitch movement (unless it is level). If there are two prominent syllables in a tone group, then the second is the tonic. The tonic here is underlined:

> **come** and look at **this**. | I **ra**ther like this **pull**over.

tone This is the movement on the tonic syllable plus any syllables that follow (sometimes called the *tail*). The tone may rise, rise-fall, fall, fall-rise or remain level. A line above the tonic marks the pitch and tone movement (see also p.20):

> **Come** and look at `**this** | I **ra**ther like this ˇ **pull**over.

pitch This is the height of the voice caused by vibrating the vocal cords. It can be high, mid or low.

Compare the intonation possibilities in B's answers:

(A: **Come** and look at **<u>this</u>** | I **ra**ther like this **<u>pull</u>**over.)

B: It's very **<u>nice</u>**. (low pitch)

B: Yes, but the ma**ter**ial's syn**<u>thet</u>**ic. (mid pitch)

B: Oh **no**, it's **<u>aw</u>**ful! (high pitch)

voice range This is the difference between the highest and lowest points of pitch in an utterance. English tends to have wider voice range than many other languages. A wide range implies some emotional involvement: the wider the range, the more emotion is being expressed.

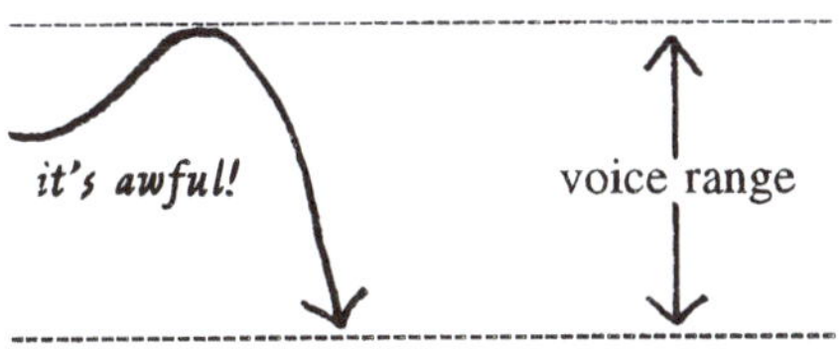

Functions of intonation

highlighting

This means the use of higher pitch, together with volume, speed and more distinct pronunciation on the tonics, to make the more important words in an utterance more prominent, as in the word *this* in the following:

come and look at **<u>this</u>**

involvement

A wide variation of pitch is used to express emotional involvement. The stronger we feel, the wider the voice range. Compare the pitch variations in the words *awful* and *synthetic* in the following:

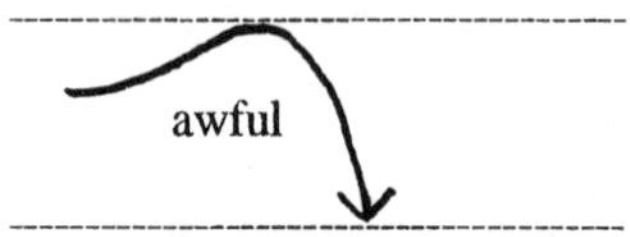

open / closed

Rising intonation expresses that something is incomplete, needs to be discussed further, resolved, confirmed etc.

O.K.?

Falling intonation indicates the end of discussion, as in strong commands:

Don't buy that one!

***shared information*: (fall)-rise**

This indicates that the information is old or already shared by the speakers.

It's very nice.

***new information:* fall**

This indicates that the information is new, being introduced by the speaker for the first time.

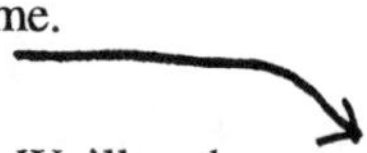

We'll go home now.

***expectations*:** falling intonation indicates expected agreement - the lower the pitch, the more confident the expected agreement.

... the material's synthetic, isn't it?

Rising intonation indicates lack of expectation - the higher the pitch, the lower the level of agreement.

You're not serious, are you?

showing care / politeness: a fall followed by a less prominent rise - a typically English pattern for showing politeness or giving a soft command.

Come on then.

reservations: this is a form of mitigation - you don't really agree but don't want to say so directly so as not to hurt someone's feelings. This could be regarded as a typically British characteristic. Here the voice starts at a high pitch, does a fall-rise, then continues with a mid-pitch. The sounds are often drawn out (i.e. lengthened) during the fall-rise phase.

Yes, but ....

grammatical: the intonation reflects the intended grammatical meaning by highlighting certain words which avoid ambiguity. In the use of defining and non-defining relative clauses we can see how the intonation parallels the use of commas in the writing in order to make the sense clear. In our dialogue the intonation of the defining relative clause does not stress *people*, making it clear that we are only talking about those people who wear yellow:

The people who wear **yel**low | are old-**fash**ioned.

If we change the intonation to that of a non-defining relative clause, it needs to stress the word *people* and have an extra tone group, making it clear that we are talking about all the people, and that *who wear yellow* is extra information:

The **peo**ple , | who wear **yel**low , | are old-**fash**ioned.

The Sounds of English · Phonetic Symbols

Consonants

p	*as in*	pig; pup
b	*as in*	big; pub
d	*as in*	dear; bad
t	*as in*	tear; bat
k	*as in*	coat; back
g	*as in*	goat; bag
ʧ	*as in*	choke; rich
ʤ	*as in*	joke; ridge
v	*as in*	view; leave
f	*as in*	few ; leaf
θ	*as in*	thin; breath
ð	*as in*	then; breathe
s	*as in*	sue; ice
z	*as in*	zoo; eyes
ʃ	*as in*	sugar; portion
ʒ	*as in*	genre; television
h	*as in*	hot; whole
m	*as in*	men; plum
n	*as in*	note; oven
ŋ	*as in*	finger; think
l	*as in*	lamp; miller
ɫ	*as in*	film; ball
r	*as in*	read; write
j	*as in*	you; union
w	*as in*	wet; question

Vowels

iː	*as in*	sheep; leap	
ɪ	*as in*	ship; lip	
i *	*as in*	happy; country	
e	*as in*	bed; said	
æ	*as in*	man; hat	
ɑː	*as in*	arm; marble	
ɒ *	*as in*	gone; orange	(Note that the symbol ɔ is now old-fashioned.)
ɔː	*as in*	author; thorn	
ʊ	*as in*	foot; should	
u *	*as in*	refugee; influence	
uː	*as in*	suit; food	
ʌ	*as in*	butter; onion	
ɜː	*as in*	word; heard	
ə	*as in*	mother	

Diphthongs

eɪ	*as in*	rain; play	
əʊ	*as in*	go; only	
ɒʊ	*as in*	old; whole	(This is used as a variant for əʊ before an 'l'.)
aɪ	*as in*	high; buy	
ɔɪ	*as in*	noise; enjoy	
ɪə	*as in*	ear; pierce	
eə	*as in*	air; pear	
ʊə	*as in*	cure; endure	

* These symbols, perhaps unfamiliar to some learners, are used not only throughout this book, but in the Longman Pronunciation Dictionary (J.C. Wells, Longman 1990) and in all up-to-date English Language reference and practice books.

N.B.: The term used to describe the form of English used throughout this book is Standard Southern British English (SSBE).

Note that, for speed and ease of reference, a diagram of the main speech organs appears on p.168 - the last page of this book.

Stress and Intonation Marks

To indicate where the stress occurs in individual words that are given in phonetic symbols in this book, a three-level system is used:

1. The vertical superscript ˈ is used to indicate strongly stressed syllables that do not carry a pitch movement – so-called **primary stress**:

exciting	ɪkˈsaitɪŋ
adjective	ˈædʒɪktɪv

2. The vertical subscript ˌ is used to indicate weakly stressed syllables – so-called **secondary stress** – in words where the primary stress is on another syllable:

satisfactory	ˌsɑtɪsˈfæktri
democratic	ˌdeməˈkrætɪk

3. **Unstressed syllables** are not marked.

To indicate the pitch movement on the tonic syllable in tone groups (see p.14), **small directional lines** (not the arrows) are used. At its shortest, a complete tone group can consist of a single, one-syllable word. Here the word *yes* is used as an example. The arrows are given here to remind you what the small directional lines mean.

Low Fall ˎ Yes

High Fall ˋ Yes

Low Rise ˏ Yes

High Rise ˊ Yes

Fall-Rise ˇ Yes

Rise-Fall ˆ Yes

Stressed syllables occurring after the tonic are indicated by the vertical subscript: ˌ

The boundaries ***between*** tone groups are indicated by a single vertical line:

It's very nice, isn't it?	ɪts veri ˎnaɪs | ˎɪznt ɪt

Unit 1 Stress Patterns

ENGLISH IS STRESSFUL!

1. Sentence stress - highlighting

1.1 When we speak we highlight meaning by raising the pitch of the stressed syllable of the important words. The voice range between the high and low points in English is often more extreme than in other languages, and if you speak in too much of a monotone you might sound bored. If there are any syllables following the highlighted syllable these fall in gradual steps:

When did you see him? -

yes
ter
I saw him day.

1.2 When the highlighted word is monosyllabic, is the last word and has a long vowel, this often glides from a high pitch to a low pitch:

Fra
We went to
ance.

About 70% of English utterances are falling at the end.

1.3 ***Listen and copy the intonation - the highlighted syllable is in bold print:***

Who did you meet?	I met **Rose**mary.
When did you meet her?	I met her on **Mon**day.
Where did you meet her?	I met her in the **cin**ema.
What's he **like**?	He's a **pain**!
Let's go to the **the**atre.	I've got nothing to **wear**.
Where's Catherine got to?	Catherine's at **home**.
How much **cheese** do you want?	I'll take a **pound**.

2. Weak Forms

2.1 *Compare the following:*

Would you like **some** tea?	Yes please, I'd love **some**.
Where do you come **from**?	I come **from** Denmark.

Notice how *some* and *from* are pronounced in a reduced, weak form when before the nouns and in a full, strong form when standing alone. The weak forms allow words with less important meaning to be spoken quickly, usually by replacing the full vowel with the schwa sound /ə/.

2.2 The following words have weak forms with the schwa.

	strong form	**weak form**	**example sentence with weak form**
to	/tuː/	/tə/	I'm going to town.
from	/frɒm/	/frəm/	I've just come home from work.
for	/fɔː/	/fə/	I'll be gone for two hours.
at	/æt/	/ət/	She's at home.
as	/æz/	/əz/	As soon as possible.
of	/ɒv/	/əv/	I'll have a cup of coffee.
can	/kæn/	/kən/	He can come too.
could	/kʊd/	/kəd/	Who could've known that?
must	/mʌst/	/məst/	Why must Tony always be the one?
should	/ʃʊd/	/ʃəd/	What should we do?

was	/wɒz/	/wəz/	She <u>was</u> eating.
has	/hæz/	/həz/	What <u>has</u> history taught us?
have	/hæv/	/həv/	What <u>have</u> you done?
had	/hæd/	/həd/	She said John <u>had</u> done it!
does	/dʌz/	/dəz/	What <u>does</u> she do?
a	/eɪ/	/ə/	I'm applying for <u>a</u> new job.
an	/æn/	/ən/	We've got <u>an</u> idea.
the	/ðiː/	/ðə/	Where's <u>the</u> nearest garage?
some	/sʌm/	/səm/	I need <u>some</u> help.
such	/sʌʧ/	/səʧ/	I've never heard <u>such</u> nonsense!
and	/ænd/	/ənd/	I'd like to bring Tony <u>and</u> Angela.
but	/bʌt/	/bət/	He's friendly <u>but</u> stupid.
than	/ðæn/	/ðən/	She's taller <u>than</u> me.
them	/ðem/	/ðəm/	Do you know <u>them</u>?
us	/ʌs/	/əs/	They gave <u>us</u> some food.
that	/ðæt/	/ðət/	Where's the pen <u>that</u> you used?
you	/juː/	/jə/	What d'<u>you</u> think of that?
your	/jɔː/	/jə/	Here's <u>your</u> money.

2.3 Contractions

A few common verb forms are mostly contracted in informal spoken English to facilitate quick speaking. Many of these contractions are probably well-known to learners because they are so commonly heard and because nowadays they are often reflected in written dialogue.

have - 've; had - 'd; would - 'd; not - n't; will - 'll; are - 're

A few of these contractions pose pronunciation problems because the full vowel is usually replaced by a schwa and sometimes (as with *n't*) by nothing. Be careful to say /v/, not /f/, in *should've, could've*, etc.

has - 's:	Giles /əz/ worked all night on the book.
have - 've:	The boys /əv/ eaten all my chocolate.
had - 'd:	John /əd/ finished it before I arrived.
should have - should've:	Harriet /ʃədəv/ done it, not you.
could have - could've:	Anyone /kədəv/ told you the answer.

would have - would’ve:	Ruth /wədəv/ come if she’d known.
would have - ’d’ve:	Maybe she /dəv/ come if he’d asked her.
are - ’re:	The kids /ə/ happy enough.
you are - you’re:	/jə/ teasing me.
my - m’:	Have you seen /mə/ wallet?
your - y’:	Where’s /jə/ car?
not - n’t:	I /hævnt/ seen that film yet.

2.4 You also find the schwa form:

- in many polysyllabic words:

Scotland	cupboard	machine	husband
doorman	Oxford	welcome	tomorrow

- in prefixes:

computer	perform	convenient	asleep

- in suffixes:

puncture	judgment	relation	poisonous

2.5 Sometimes the unstressed vowel sound becomes an /ɪ/ sound:

became	carried	eleven
exam	example	expect
goodness	private	repeat
return	village	women

3. Stress-timed language

3.1 English is a stress-timed language, which means that the stress beats (the stressed syllables) follow each other at roughly regular intervals. If you say the following numbers, notice how the extra syllable in *seven* does not disturb the stress pattern because here it is a weak form and said very quickly:

one, two, three, four, five
six, sev(en), eight, nine, ten

3.2 In order to achieve the rhythm of spoken English as a stress-timed language, the words that carry meaning are stressed, and the other words have a reduced or weak pronunciation. As the number of syllables between the main beats is variable, this means that the more syllables there are between the beats the more quickly they have to be pronounced so that the rhythm is not lost. The weak forms allow the phrases with more syllables to be spoken more quickly.

Three			**blind**		**mice**			
Three			**blind**		**mice**			
See			**how**	they	**run**			
See			**how**	they	**run**			
They	**all**	ran	**after**	the	**far**mer's		**wife**	
Who	**cut**	off their	**tails**	with a	**car**ving		**knife**	
Did you	**ever**		**see**	such a	**thing**	in your	**life**	as
three			**blind**		**mice** ?			

Now practise this rhythm with the following examples:

3.3 There **was** a young **per**son from **Perth**,
Who was **born** on the **day** of his **birth**,
He was **mar**ried, they **say**,
On his **wife's** wedding **day**,
And **died** when he **quit**ted this **earth**.

3.4 A: We're **com**ing on the **twen**tieth of **June**.
B: **Will** you be **stay**ing for the **par**ty?
A: Oh, I'm not **sure**, but I'll **be** there if I **can**.

4. Dialogue: On the Phone

Dramatis Personae:

Gareth: *aged 32, a short Maths teacher who is rather feeble and lacking in confidence, and has little sense of irony.*

Heather: *a tall, blonde, 30-year-old woman, rather forceful, and keen on male company whatever the cost.*

Heather:	Bexleyheath 602332.
Gareth:	I'd like to speak to Catherine.
Heather:	Cath's not at home tonight. Who's that?
Gareth:	Er, I'm a friend of Cath's ...
Heather:	Oh, you must be Matthew.
Gareth:	No, I'm Gareth. Who's Matthew?
Heather:	Cath's got two heartthrobs at the moment - one's a tall, handsome businessman from Sevenoaks and the other is a short, fat, impoverished teacher from Brixton. Gareth, where do you come from?
Gareth:	And what's wrong with Brixton? Anyway, who are you?
Heather:	I'm Cath's older sister, Heather. I'm sorry to break the bad news, Gareth, but my wicked sister has been two-timing you.
Gareth:	Oh no! I've got two tickets for the theatre tomorrow. I thought she might be interested.
Heather:	Why don't you take me instead? I love going to the theatre, you know. What's on?
Gareth:	But I don't know you.
Heather:	That's a strange title! Who wrote it?
Gareth:	Shakespeare - it's that Scottish play, you know.
Heather:	What's Macbeth got to do with "But I don't know you"?
Gareth:	Oh dear, it must be Monday!

5. Exercises

5.1 Limerick

Complete this limerick. Practise saying it with the correct intonation.

There was a young student from Spain,
Who came to England by train,

5.2

SLEUTHMAN

Listen to the interview between Sleuthman*, the world-famous private detective, and a journalist from Crime magazine.

Journalist: *Mr. Sleuthman, your office here in the backstreets of Lewisham, South London, is really small, I must say.*

Sleuthman: *Oh, yes, deliberately so. Firstly, the smaller the office, the easier it is to keep tidy. This means I throw away everything that isn't absolutely essential.*

Journalist: *Oh, I see. But why do you work in such a run-down area?*

Sleuthman: *Well, the nature of crime here means I have easy access to underground sources and I can keep up-to-date with the latest criminal methods.*

Journalist: *Very interesting. What has been your most successful case so far?*

Sleuthman: *Well, unfortunately the number of cases I deal with has been falling. Er, let me see. There's the case of industrial espionage that I solved.*

Journalist: *Ah, the one at British Nuclear Fuels.*

Sleuthman: *No, the one at Gertie's Ice Cream Parlour down the road. The Italian mafia stole her recipe for Worcester-sauce-flavoured ice cream.*

Journalist: *Oh, you mean the case last year that we all read about in the tabloids?*

Sleuthman: *No, no, you never read about the successful cases in the press!*

Journalist: *I see. Well there's no point in pressing you further. Thank you for your valuable time. I'm sure this area is safer due to your presence. Goodbye.*

Sleuthman: *Goodbye. Mind you don't get mugged on the way out!*

**Sleuth* is a humorous word for a detective.

5.3 ***Make sentences with these jumbled words. Underline the weak / reduced forms /ə/ or /ɪ/, and use a highlighter pen to pick out the strong forms. (Don't forget contractions). Then check your answers in the key.***

1. he / come / can / too
2. she / must / mad / agree / to / been / to / that / have
3. poison / effective / as / this / one / isn't / as / that
4. author / where / not / I'm / comes / at / sure / all / the / from / know / I
5. I / computer / would / have / on / exam / the / done / the
6. she / do / as / can / well / it / just / he / as / can
7. you / do / for / that / did / what?
8. do / ironing / the / I / do / to / have?

5.4 ***Matthew's Room***

Look at this picture of Matthew's room. On the cassette you hear statements about where things are situated. Give two answers, and try to copy the pattern of highlighting.

e.g. statement: The vase is on the desk.
answer 1: No, the vase is under the table.
answer 2: The cup is on the desk.

(1) statement: The poster is above the desk.
answer 1:
answer 2:

(2) statement: The bag is on the chair.
answer 1:
answer 2:

(3) statement: The lamp is on the bedside table.
answer 1:
answer 2:

(4) statement: The books are under the bed.
answer 1:
answer 2:

(5) statement: The scissors are under the desk.
answer 1:
answer 2:

5.5 ***Go back to the Sleuthman text. Listen to it again and mark the highlighted syllables to show the main stresses. The first two speeches have been done for you:***

Journalist: Mr. Sleuthman, your office here in the backstreets of Lewisham, South London, is really small, I must say.

Sleuthman: Oh, yes, deliberately so. Firstly, the smaller the office, the easier it is to keep tidy. This means I throw away everything that isn't absolutely essential.

Unit 2 Linking: Where‿is‿it?

THE MISSING LINK!

Linking is a fundamental part of speaking English. If you don't link your words in the correct way, your English will sound abrupt and staccato. Understanding the rules of linking is the first step towards sounding more natural.

1. Linking rules

1.1 Consonants + vowel

When a word ends in a consonant and the next begins with a vowel, then the two words are usually linked smoothly in naturally spoken English:

Listen and speak:

Come‿in! She's‿at home. When‿is‿it? I'm‿in‿England.
He's‿an‿amazing‿artist. It's‿an‿incredible‿admission.
She's‿on‿an‿expedition.

Think of this last consonant as the beginning of the next word:

Goo dafternoon Goo devening a norange Wha tisit?

1.2 /r/ + vowel

(a) Linking /r/

An /r/ is pronounced at the end of a word if the next word begins with a vowel:

our‿uncle at your‿age they're‿outside her‿older‿animals car‿engine

Listen to the dialogue and mark in the linking:

Visitor:	I'd like to see Mr. Andrews or a colleague of his.
Secretary:	Sorry, but they're all in a meeting.
Visitor:	But here is a rather urgent letter for your accounts department.
Secretary:	Their office is at the far end of the corridor.
Visitor:	Thank you for your assistance.

(b) Intrusive /r/

When a word ending in /ɔː/, /ə/ or /ɑː/ is followed by a word starting with a vowel, then the two words are often linked with an /r/ sound in modern English. The same phenomenon occurs across the hyphen in hyphenated words:

after ɔː	I saw/r/it	awe-/r/inspiring
after ə	Emma/r/and Bob	law-/r/abiding
after ɑː	Grandma/r/and grandad	The idea/r/of‿it!

1.3 A /j/ sound is often added to link the following vowel sounds:

after iː	the/j/author	we/j/are here
after eɪ	ray/j/of hope	they/j/are coming
after i	Happy/j/anniversary!	very/j/interesting
after ɔɪ	boy/j/and girl	Enjoy/j/it!
after aɪ	Why/j/is‿it?	by/j/all‿accounts

1.4 A /w/ sound is added to link the following vowel sounds:

after uː	you/w/are	a new‿office
after aʊ	How‿old are you?	Now‿only three remained.
after əʊ	so/w/interesting	Go/w/and tell him.

Remember that the pronunciation of 'u' at the beginning of some words is /juː/, e.g. *university, unification, unanimous*. There is no linking to words in this category.

the uncle	**ði**‿ʌŋkl	but	*the university*	**ðə** juːnəˈvɜːsəti
an unavoidable decision /ʌ/		but	*a unanimous decision* /juː/	

1.5 *We also often link over commas when reading:*

in tag questions: She's‿an intelligent **woman,‿isn't** she?

after *yes* and *no*: **No,‿/w/I** didn't say that.
Yes,‿I‿agree.

after interjections: **Oh,‿/w/I‿**am surprised to hear that.
Ah,‿/r/I thought‿it was you.

1.6 *Mark in the linking in all of the following. Practise speaking the questions and responses, paying attention to the linking.*

Questions / statements	**Possible responses**
Where are Arthur and Rick?	They're on holiday.
What's the answer?	I've got no idea.
Your umbrella is awful!	You ought to buy another.
Leave our toys alone!	Why should I? These aren't your only toys.

Do stay a while!	Sorry, I've got to be off now.
There's a knock at the door.	Well, go and see who it is, then.
Why don't you ask them?	They're too upset to ask.
Can I help you at all, madam?	Yes, there's a flaw in this material.
Who have you invited?	Anna and Richard, and Celia and Ron.
I arrest you in the name of the law.	But I'm a law-abiding citizen!

1.7 Tongue Twister

Say the tongue twister several times out loud, paying attention to the linking.

Q: What noise annoys an oyster?

A: A noisy noise annoys an oyster.

2. Dialogue: Gareth and Heather at the Theatre

Gareth: Are you enjoying the Shakespearean acting, Heather?

Heather: Sssh! You'll annoy other people. I'd rather exchange opinions in the interval, if you don't mind.

Gareth: But it *is* the interval.

Heather: So it is. Let's go and buy a glass of wine or champagne at the bar.

Gareth: That's a good idea. My throat is beginning to cry out for a drink.

Heather: What a peculiar expression! You've got a very odd way of speaking, I must say. You're almost poetic.

Gareth: Ah, if only other people appreciated me in the same way. But your sister thinks I'm a bore and she says she'd rather I didn't ask her out any more.

Heather: You ought to leave her alone then. There are other fish in the sea, after all. Like me, for instance.

Gareth: Oh Heather, you've got no idea how much I love her. She's my inspiration, my life, my everything.

Heather: Now you're overdoing it, Gareth. You sound like a bad song. There's the bell. Shall we go in again?

Gareth: Oh you women are all the same: so insensitive and so unemotional.

3. Exercises

3.1 ***Here are 10 uses for an ostrich egg! Mark in the links, then repeat all ten, concentrating on the linking:***

1. Break it open and count the yolks.
2. Put it under Aunt Eva's cushion.
3. Sit on it until it hatches out.
4. Use it as a paper weight.
5. Break it into a frying pan.
6. Make a big egg cup and put it inside.
7. Cook it and eat it.
8. Paint a picture on it and hang it up.
9. Plant it in the garden - will it grow?
10. Shoot at it with an air gun.

3.2 ***Write down five uses for one of the following, using as many examples of linking as you can. Practise saying them aloud.***

a paper aeroplane   *an empty ashtray*   *a yellow umbrella*

1. ....
2. ....
3. ....
4. ....
5. ....

3.3 *Mark in the linking in the following text. Practise speaking:*

SLEUTHMAN

Sleuthman came into the restaurant at one o'clock. Janet was staring into her empty glass, still attempting to work out the answer to the puzzle. Surely Amanda and Dickie couldn't have carried the body 500 yards on their own? Sleuthman came over and tapped her on the arm. "Wake up, my dear. It's too early for sleeping - it's time for action!" "Oh, Monsieur, you gave me a shock! I think I'm too upset to assist you."

3.4 *Why is Janet upset? Write an ending for the story, using as many different forms of linking as you can. Now practise reading your story aloud.*

....

....

....

....

....

3.5 Alphabet

1. ***Can you say the alphabet? And backwards?***

2. ***How do you spell ... ?*** Write down the names of three famous people. Then read the spellings out loud.

3.6 Homophones

English is a language rich in homophones: a homophone is a word that sounds the same as another but has a different spelling and meaning,

e.g. no - know.

What are the homophones here? What are the spellings and meanings?

1. by 1_______ 2_______
2. rain 1_______ 2_______
3. so 1_______ 2_______
4. vein 1_______ 2_______
5. sores 1_______ 2_______
6. or 1_______ 2_______ 3_______
7. I'll 1_______ 2_______

8. week _______
9. nor _______
10. blue _______
11. rose _______
12. metre _______
13. new _______
14. which _______
15. pain _______
16. desert (vb.) _______
17. sauce _______
18. plane _______
19. heir _______

3.7 ***Here are some expressions in phonetic script with no gaps, as they would normally be spoken in natural conversation. Can you say them? Pay particular attention to the weak forms.***

1. ˈmɪlkənˎʃʊgə
2. ˈhɑːfpɑːs t ˎeɪt
3. ˈfaɪvtəˎnaɪn
4. səmˈbredn ˎbʌtə
5. ˈaɪmfrəmʤəˎpæn
6. əzˈkwɪkəzəˎflæʃ

3.8 **Joke Time!**

Do you get these jokes?

1. ˋdɒktə | ˋdɒktə | aɪ ˈfiːl laɪk ə ˈpeər əv ˎkɜːtnz
   ˈpʊl jəˈself təˎgeðə ˌmæn.
2. ˈwɒts ˈdrækjələz ˈfeɪvrɪt ˎpʊdɪŋ?
   aɪˎskriːm.
3. ˈwɒts ðə ˇdɪfrəns | bɪˈtwiːn ə ˈwet ˏdeɪ | ənd ə ˈlaɪən wɪð ˎtuːθeɪk?
   ˈwʌn ˈpɔːz wɪð ˏreɪn | ən ði ˈʌðə ˈrɔːz wɪð ˎpeɪn.
4. ˎtiːʧəː jɔː ˎleɪt | ju ˈʃʊd əv bɪn ˈhɪər ət ˈnaɪnə ˎklɒk
   ˎbɔɪː ˋwaɪ mɪs | ˈwɒt ˋhæpnd?
5. ˈwaɪ dɪd ðə ˏbɔɪ | ˌθrəʊ ðə ˈklɒk ˌaʊt əv ðə ˎwɪndəʊ?
   tə ˈsiː ˈtaɪm ˎflaɪ.

Unit 3 /θ/ thin /ð/ then

AN UDDER MILK SHAKE, PLEASE

The 'th' sounds are very important in English, because if you do not pronounce them correctly you will often be misunderstood:

I have no **faith** (not *face* or *fate*).
I can't **breathe** (not *breeze* or *breed*).

1. Listening

1.1 *Which is the odd one out?*

You will hear four words being spoken. You then have to decide which of the four is being pronounced differently. For example, if you hear:

1	2	3	4
faith	*faith*	*face*	*faith* ,

then the third word has been pronounced differently, so that is the odd one out and the answer is 3. The first answer is already given to you below.

a. 3 b. c. d. e.

1.2 *Which word(s) is / are correct?*

You will hear groups of words being spoken. When you hear a 'th' sound, tick the appropriate column(s) (✓). For example, with *thin*, if you hear *thin thin sin thin,* then you tick columns 1, 2 and 4.

	1.	2.	3.	4.
a. thin				
b. thick				
c. other				
d. worth				
e. breathe				
f. clothing				
g. there				

2. Articulation

Native speakers actually place the tip of the tongue lightly against the upper teeth. If you are an advanced learner, or very confident, or both, you can do the same. However, for the vast majority of learners, the best tip is to put the tongue ***through the teeth***. Blow air between your tongue and the upper teeth.
Say ***thin.***

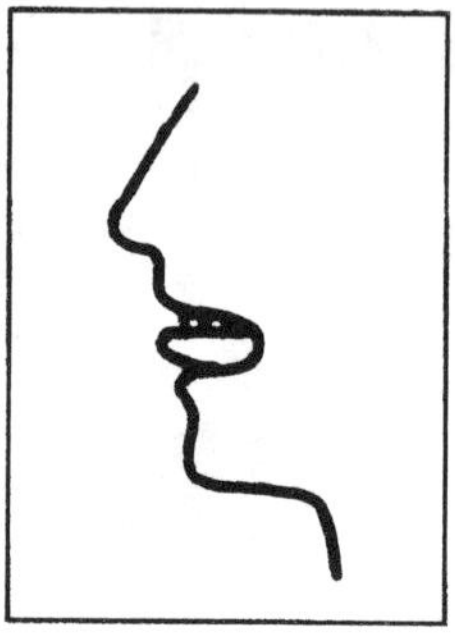

/θ/ and /ð/ - best tongue position for most learners

For the voiced /ð/, use your voice to produce vibration.
Say ***then.***
Warning!
Don't say /s/ or /t/ for /θ/: say ***thin***, not *sin* or *tin.*
Don't say /d/ or /z/ for /ð/: say ***then***, not *den* or *Zen.*

3. /θ/ and /ð/

Both of these sounds can occur in any position in a word: initial, medial or final. Since it is not possible to give hard-and-fast rules about when to use which, you should make it a high priority to learn which of the two sounds occurs in the most common words:

Initial position:

voiced /ð/:

the, this, then, though, these, those, than, that, there

voiceless /θ/:

three, throw, through, thwart (i.e. especially before /r/ and /w/);
thank, theology, thin, theatre, thought, thud

Medial position:

voiced /ð/ in most cases between vowels: *father, weather, other, rather*
voiceless /θ/ in exceptional cases: *anthem, Anthea, Arthur*

Final position:

voiceless /θ/ in most cases: *month, both, cloth, north*
voiced /ð/ in some cases, and **always** in the ending '–th<u>e</u>':
bathe, booth, breathe, clothe (vb.), lithe, loathe, smooth, with
In some cases /θ/ becomes /ð/ in the plural: *mouth - mouths*

4. Listen and Speak

4.1 *Listen to the cassette and repeat, making the distinctions clear:*

sank	-	thank	Zen	-	then
torn	-	thorn	dare	-	their
Pesos	-	pathos	closing	-	clothing
martyr	-	Martha	wordy	-	worthy
mouse	-	mouth	breeze	-	breathe
fate	-	faith	load	-	loathe

4.2 *Listen to the cassette and practise speaking:*

the voiceless /θ/:

theme	thief	thought	thing	33,333
author	athletic	method	lethal	pathetic
bath	south	earth	youth	health

the voiced /ð/:

then	this	those	there	though
father	other	northern	southern	weather
with	smooth	breathe	loathe	booth

4.3 Tongue Twisters

Arthur and Kenneth threw the leather cloth hither and thither.

Did Thelma dither whether to play the zither, or did Heather dither whether to play the zither?

4.4 **"th" clusters** These are often difficult to pronounce because of the combinations of /s/ and /z/ with /θ/ and /ð/ sounds.

Listen and repeat:

/θ/ + /s/ months - births - lengths - cloths - fifths
/ð/ + /z/ breathes - soothes - mouths - loathes - clothes
/s/ + /θ/ this thing - sixth - nice thoughts
horse thief - ice thaw

Note that a normally voiced /z/, as in *his, these,* becomes /s/ under the influence of a following voiceless consonant:

/s/ + /θ/ his thumb - these three - she's thin - those theories

/s/ + /ð/ Pass the sauce - What's this? - What's the time? - Face the facts.
/z/ + /ð/ Who's that? - Is that you over there? - What's this, though?
Here's the boss! - The car's his, then?

Don't forget the secret of success:

5. Dialogue: Gareth bumps into Heather in Woolworth's during a free period.

Listen to this dialogue twice. The first time you should mark the voiced /ð/ forms and underline the highlighted syllables. Then speak the two roles, concentrating on the "th" sounds and the highlighted syllables:

Heather: Gareth! What on earth are you doing here at 11.30 on a Thursday morning?

Gareth: Buying Cath a birthday card.

Heather: I thought you'd be teaching maths to 3C.

Gareth: That was the third lesson. The fourth's free so I popped out - I needed a breath of fresh air.

Heather: In Woolworth's?

Gareth: My enthusiasm was withering in the face of slothful youths.

Heather: Oh, you poor thing!

Gareth: Thanks for the sympathy. This morning I was dictating notes on the theories of Pythagoras to the fifth year when .....

Heather: Dictating? Your nineteenth century methods need rethinking Gareth! Are you worthy of your pupils' faith in their mentor?

Gareth: ..... when they started throwing their books of logarithms at each other and me.

Heather: The thankless little good-for-nothings! That's the result of this trendy anti-authoritarian nonsense.

6. Exercises

6.1 ***Make up two tongue twisters with as many voiced and unvoiced "th" sounds as you can include. Make sure you can say it at a natural speed! Write in <u>pencil</u> first to give yourself a chance to correct or change things later.***

e.g. Keith Booth's hyacinth was withering within the thorny thicket.

1. ....

....

2. ....

....

6.2 ***Match the two halves of these proverbs. Mark which "th" sounds are voiced and which are voiceless. What do the proverbs mean? Do you agree with their sentiments?***

1. Too many cooks	a. to catch a thief.
2. Don't throw the baby	b. that help themselves.
3. Birds of a feather	c. gathers no moss.
4. God helps those	d. out with the bathwater.
5. Set a thief	e. flock together.
6. A rolling stone	f. spoil the broth.

6.3 ***Here are some typical English names. Arrange them into boys' names, girls' names and surnames. Some can be both first names and surnames, so you can list them twice. Within each of these three categories, split them further into columns with a voiceless "th" in the name and those with a voiced "th".***

Heather	*Heath*	*Agatha*	*Judith*	*Elizabeth*	*Worthington*
North	*Thelma*	*Keith*	*Thurber*	*Kenneth*	*Anthea*
Howarth	*Sutherland*	*Edith*	*Ruth*	*Arthur*	*Fotherington*
Booth	*Timothy*	*Atherton*	*Martha*	*Ethel*	*Weatherspoon*

Girls' names		Boys' names		Surnames	
/θ/	/ð/	/θ/	/ð/	/θ/	/ð/

6.4 ***Are the plurals of the following words voiced or voiceless? Check in your dictionary. Practise saying them.***

month path myth mouth hearth cloth death

6.5 ***What are the verb forms of the following nouns? How are they pronounced? Check in your dictionary.***

wreath cloth breath teeth

6.6

SLEUTHMAN

Listen to the recording of this short extract from a Sleuthman story:

Sleuthman thumped hard on the front door of Fotherington Hall. Having run up the path, he was already out of breath and sprayed his mouth with the inhaler. "This damned asthma!", he cursed. Eventually, the chained door creaked open and the owner, Bruce Thackery, thrust his head through the gap.

"Ah, Inspector Sleuthman. Thanks for coming so promptly despite this filthy weather." Sleuthman followed him through the lengthy, gloomy corridor to the drawing room.

"What did the thief take?"

"Thieves, Inspector Sleuthman - there were three of them. They took three priceless paintings by Sutherland. There was nothing I could do - they threatened to slit my throat with a knife."

"They'll either have gone north to Heathrow Airport or south on the M3 to Portsmouth. We've set up road blocks. What about you?"

"Oh, I'll be O.K. I'm a bit shaken and I think they've broken my thumb."

"Sit down, breathe deeply and try to relax, Mr Thackery. I'm just going to look for some clues."

6.7 ***Listen again to the Sleuthman text and underline the highlighted syllables to show stress. The first two sentences have been done for you:***

Sleuthman thumped hard on the front door of Fotherington Hall. Having run up the path, he was already out of breath and sprayed his mouth with the inhaler.

6.8 ***Record yourself speaking the "Sleuthman" text onto a cassette. Concentrate especially on the "th" sounds and sentence stress. Then listen to yourself critically, comparing yourself with the original recording.***

6.9 ***Arrange the words from Sleuthman with "th" sounds into the appropriate column, according to whether they are voiced or voiceless. There is one word where the "th" is not normally pronounced at all! Write this at the bottom.***

/ð/ Fotherington	/θ/ Sleuthman

Word where the "th" is not normally pronounced at all: ....

6.10 ***Fill in the gaps in the dialogue with the words from the following list. Practise saying it aloud, concentrating on the "th" forms:***

three	-	*thundery*	-	*north*	-	*weather*	-	*breathe*
whether	-	*northerly*	-	*Thursday*	-	*healthy*	-	*thicker*

Keith: What's the__________forecast for this__________?

Thora: ________showers and a force________wind, it says in the paper.

Keith: Does it say__________that's a southerly or__________wind?

Thora: From the______. We'll have to put on__________clothes.

Keith: Yes, but the cold keeps you_________ - I can't _________in this heat!

6.11 Sounds Maze

Here is a word maze using the phonemic symbols. Find at least 20 words which have a "th" sound in them. You are allowed to turn corners!

b	r	iː	ð	ɪ	ŋ
ɑː	ɒ	θ	ɔː	t	ɪ
θ	r	iː	z	əʊ	ð
r	ɑː	n	θ	r	əʊ
ə	ð	e	w	θ	l
m	ə	ð	ɪ	r	k

Unit 4 /r/ right /l/ light

WHY ARE YOU ROLLING YOUR R's?

/ɑːz/ not /ɑːs/!

A rolled 'r', whether lingual (i.e. rolled with the tip of the tongue) or uvular (i.e. rolled at the back of the mouth) will not prevent you from being understood, but will give your English a strong foreign accent.
In this unit we will practise the 'r' and 'l' sounds.

1. Listening

1.1 *Which is the odd one out?*

a. b. c. d.

1.2 *Where is the /r/ sound?*

In the following groups of words you will hear some linked together with an /r/ sound. Whenever you hear the linking /r/, tick the appropriate column.

	1.	2.	3.	4.
a.				
b.				
c.				
d.				
e.				

2. Articulation of /r/

Open your mouth slightly. Make a long /ɜː/ sound, as in *shirt*. Keeping your mouth in this position, put the tip of your tongue on the alveolar ridge to make /l/. Now take the tongue tip off the ridge ***a little bit*** and say /ɜː/ again while curling your tongue tip upwards and backwards. The /ɜː/ changes to /r/. Both lips move forward a little. The sound comes from the front of the mouth. This is the correct position to start saying *red.*

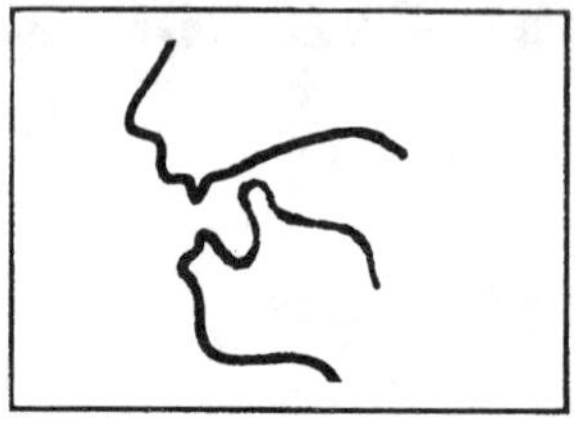

/r/

red	ready	readiness	all	already	alright

3. Listen and Speak

3.1

ring	rose	wrong	right
ferry	touring	terrible	during
cricket	street	drink	bring
Robert	Richard	Mary	Laura

N.B. In Br.E. (unlike Am.E.), the /r/ is *not* pronounced in words ending in an 'r' or 're':

car	/kɑː/	fur	/fɜː/	more	/mɔː/
her	/hɜː/	Arthur	/ˈɑːθə/	you're	/jɔː/

3.2. Linking /r/:

our‿uncle	far‿away	their‿aims	her‿arm
we're‿O.K.	poor‿Adam!	their‿aunt	car‿engine

You're‿under‿age.　　I'm sure‿of it.

3.3 Tongue Twisters

Around the rugged rocks the ragged rascal ran.

Red lorry, yellow lorry, red lorry, yellow lorry.

4. Forms of 'l'

There are two spoken forms of 'l' in English. You won't be misunderstood if you confuse them or if you use only one form, but it will not sound natural.

clear l	-	before vowels as in *lamp*
dark ɫ	-	before consonants as in *film* in final position as in *all* as a syllabic consonant as in *little*

A dark ɫ becomes clear when it is linked to the next word: eg spill‿over

N.B. the English dark ɫ is not as dark as the Russian ɫ.

Note also the silent 'l', as in *almond, colonel, half, palm, salmon, yolk.*

4.1 *Listening:*

Underline the words with a dark ɫ as you listen to the following list:

well, talk, less, mild, lips, soul, psalm, sold, folk

4.2 ***Which is the odd one out?***

a. b. c. d.

5. Articulation of ɫ

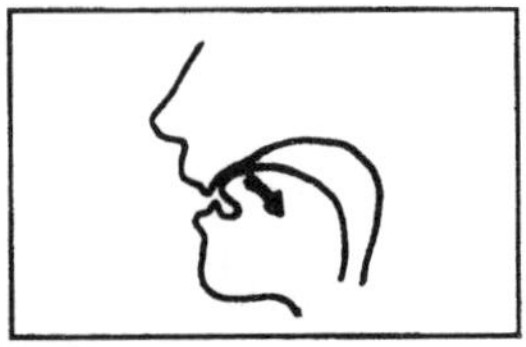

clear l

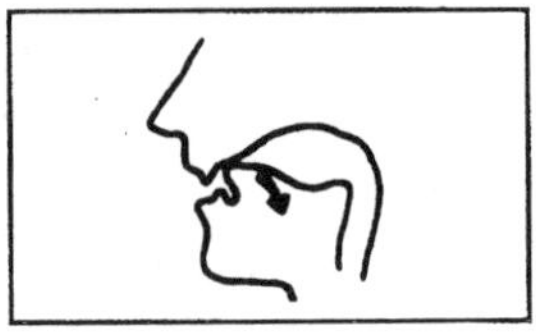

dark ɫ

The tip of the tongue is on the alveolar ridge.
The tongue should be relaxed (more than for the clear l).
The back of the tongue should be raised a little: say əl.
But remember: when the ɫ at the end of a word is followed by a word beginning with a vowel, it becomes a clear l (see **4.** above.)

5.1 ***Listen and Speak:***

ɫ:	fill	tell	cool	pull	steal	mill	sail
l:	filler	telling	cooler	pulley	stealing	miller	sailing
ɔːɫ	ball	fall	bald	hall	tall	called	
əʊɫ:	bowl	foal	bold	hold	toll	cold	
ɫ:	Bill	Beryl	Hazel	Jill	Carl	Dale	Neil
ɫ → l:	fill - fill it in		call - call it a day			all - all I want	

5.2 **Limericks** ***Which 'l' is being used in each case?***

A wonderful bird is the pelican:
His bill can hold more
than his belican.
He can take in his beak
Food enough for a week,
But I'm damned if I see
how the helican!

There was a young man called Paul
Who went to a fancy dress ball.
He thought he could risk it
To go as a biscuit,
But a dog ate him up in the hall!

6. Syllabic Consonants: ɫ metal ɫ medal

There are two ways of saying some syllables beginning with a /d/ or /t/ and followed by ɫ. With syllabic ɫ the air is passed out at the sides of the tongue. Thus 'metal' can be pronounced either 'metəɫ (with a normal weak form at the end) or metɫ (with a syllabic 'l').
In natural, spoken English, the syllabic consonant is more common.

6.1 *Listening: syllabic ɫ or əɫ?*

metal, middle, kettle, bottle, little, riddle, paddle, fickle

6.2 *Listen and Speak:*

əɫ: cattle battle medal bottle settle gentle fatal
ɫ: cattle battle medal bottle settle gentle fatal
əɫ: kettle, idle, middle, double, apple, people, uncle, article, eagle
ɫ: kettle, idle, middle, double, apple, people, uncle, article, eagle
tɫ: We drank a bottle of nettle wine.

7. Word stress in two-syllable words

7.1 *Where are the following (and most) two-syllable words stressed?*

hero	helping	English	practice	action	feudal
hopeful	stanza	chapter	linguist	system	poker
novel	chimney	poet	finger	sauna	actress

7.2 ***Where is the stress if the second syllable has a long vowel or ends in two consonants?***

around	Japan	alive	afraid	refuse	succeed	machine
correct	attract	prevent	respect	indent	corrupt	refresh

Unfortunately, there are some exceptions to the rules:

athlete, **com**merce, **pre**fect, Ber**lin**,* **phy**sics, **chal**lenge, ho**tel***

* See Unit 12 for more information on how the stress of these words changes when the words form part of a compound.

8. Word stress with prefixes

8.1 ***Where is the primary stress in these words beginning with a prefix?***

important	became	conclude	uncertain
understand	response	illegal	defrost

8.2 *Question:* **How many prefixes in 8.1 are stressed?**
Answer: **None: prefixes rarely carry primary stress.***

*But see **8.3** for an important exception to this.

This should especially be remembered in opposite or negation forms with prefixes:

un**hap**py, impo**lite**, il**le**gal, disap**point**, mis**trust**, ir**rel**evant, incor**rect**

8.3 ***There is a group of words in English that can be used as nouns / adjectives or verbs. Can you work out the stress rules from these examples? The stressed syllables are in bold print.***

a. The **ex**port of arms was banned.
They ex**port** arms to the Third World.

b. Do you still subscribe to *The Reader's* ***Di****gest*?
He's quite ill - he can't di**gest** his food properly.

c. She thanked him for the lovely **pre**sent.
The manager will pre**sent** the report tomorrow.

The noun / adjective forms are stressed on the **first** syllable: ˈ**ex**port
The verb forms are stressed on the **second** syllable: exˈ**port**

Notice how the first syllable changes into a weak form /ə/ or /ɪ/ when it is not stressed.

Mark in the primary stress in the underlined words in these four sentences:

1. The strikers refuse to go back to work without better conditions.
2. We always take our refuse to the dump at the weekend.
3. We don't frequent the local theatre as much as we should do.
4. They are frequent visitors to Dartmoor.

9. Dialogue: Gareth calls round at Cath's house with a bunch of roses.

Heather: Gareth, what lovely roses, such an unusual orange. Thanks very much.
Gareth: Er, sorry Heather, actually I rather thought Cath might appreciate them. Orange is her favourite colour, or so she tells me.
Heather: You really do spoil my little sister rotten. Well, come into the living room.
Gareth: Is Cath in her room?
Heather: No, she's staying with our Auntie Myrtle and she won't return till tomorrow. Surely you remember that?
Gareth: All I know is Cath promised to go to the ball with me this evening.
Heather: Well Gareth, it looks as if you're out of luck...unless you're able to find a replacement.
Gareth: All my friends are going. Oh dear, what would you recommend?
Heather: You could always try asking me to go to the ball.
Gareth: But you're so tall. How can we rock 'n' roll if I can't reach your shoulder?

10. Exercises

10.1 ***Make up a tongue twister with as many /ɹ/ sounds as possible - practise saying the tongue twister until the /ɹ/ sounds are near-perfect.***

10.2 ***Practise reading the dialogue "Gareth calls round to Cath's house with a bunch of roses" onto a cassette and listen to yourself critically!***

10.3 ***What are the basic stress rules for two-syllable words?***

10.4 ***Complete the following words by putting one or two 'l's in each gap. Mark the stresses and practise saying the words aloud. Check in your dictionary if you are not sure of any of the words.***

rebe__ion	a __ready	beautifu__	wonderfu__
para__e__	farewe__	meta__ic	we__come
fai__ed	boi__ed	tota__y	tota__ity
woo__en	a__ways	marve__ed	quarre__ed
contro__ed	sai__ed	rebe__ed	jewe__er
nove__ist	coo__er	boi__er	tranqui__

10.5 ***Mark the stress in these words, then practise saying them.***

essay	accent	system	active	passive	decade	chimney	design
margin	ruler	social	career	method	although	humane	engine
syntax	enter	equal	assist	envy	balloon	persuade	exam
justice	human	hotel	satire	sandal	repair	perform	motor

10.6 ***Can you do the dark ɫ in near-perfect fashion? Practise with the following words:***

ball - metal - little - film - article - cool - cold - called

10.7 ***Cross out the silent letters in the following words and practise saying them.***

debt	psychology	knife	answer	itinerary	lamb
receipt	psychiatrist	whole	preferable	hour	walk
knead	contemporary	subtle	honest	wrong	doubt
library	pneumonia	psalm	thumb	salmon	dumb
iron	vegetable	almond	wreck	gnome	comfortable

10.8 ***Fill in the gaps with the appropriate word from the list below. Mark the primary stress in these words, and practise speaking them.***

escort	**insult**	**rebel**	**progress**	**permit**
produce	**desert**	**subject**	**perfect**	**object**

1. He walked across the____________in the heat of the day.
2. I wouldn't _____________ to having more holidays.
3. Most young people feel the need to____________ against their parents.
4. To be called lazy is a bit of an____________ .
5. The professor wouldn't_________the students to talk during her lecture.
6. Some people believe it is necessary to____________ animals to pain for science to make ____________.
7. The farmers sold their fresh______________ at the market.
8. A little more work is needed to____________ this model.
9. The prison warder was ordered to_____________ the prisoner to his cell.

10.9 ***Write in the opposites of the following words by adding an appropriate prefix. Mark the stresses and practise saying them. Look them up in a dictionary if you are not sure of how they are pronounced.***

official -	real -	acceptable -
logical -	satisfied -	honest -
legible -	possible -	trustful -
efficient -	reasonable -	effective -
transitive -	afraid -	mature -
correct -	patient -	obedient -

10.10 ***Fill in the missing words in these proverbs from the list below. Are there equivalents in your language? What do they mean? Practise saying them.***

absence	**sweep**	**Rome**	**doubt**	**silk**
fire	**mountain**	**while**	**contempt**	**silver**

1. Don't make a ______________out of a molehill.
2. You can't make a_________purse out of a sow's ear.
3. When in________, leave it out.
4. _________wasn't built in a day.
5. Every cloud has a _________lining.
6. Make hay__________ the sun shines.
7. Familiarity breeds ___________________ .
8. New brooms__________________ clean.
9. ______________ makes the heart grow fonder.
10. There's no smoke without a ____________ .

Make sure you know all the meanings.

10.11 ***Can you read these sentences?***

(i) hiz ə ˇnɜːv ˌspeʃəlɪst | hu 'præktɪsɪz ˌsaɪkəʊə ˋnæləsɪs

(ii) 'ðɪs 'kɔːts ˏvɜːdɪkt | wəz ə 'mɪskærɪʤ əv ˎʤʌstɪs

(iii) 'ɑːntʃu 'glæd ðət ðɪs 'həʊmwɜːks 'ɔːlməʊs kəmˏpliːtɪd?

10.12

SLEUTHMAN

Listen to the story about Sleuthman's lousy rotten day. Mark in the highlighted syllables and practise speaking. Record yourself when you think you are perfect, and compare your version with the original.

What a miserable rainy Friday! Everything was going wrong. Sleuthman's alarm clock failed to go off, he leapt out of bed and fell on the floor, bruising his skull on the table. There was no milk in the fridge so he had to eat his favourite breakfast cereal dry. Rover, his bulldog, greeted him with a friendly lick, but nothing could calm Sleuthman's ragged nerves on this terrible morning.

Having arrived late at work, he received a phone call from his secretary, who rang to say she was ill. He screamed, "Oh no! Now I'll have to do all the boring filing myself."

Right at that moment, a rather angry-looking man walked into the office. "Hey mister," he growled, "I need your assistance to help solve a crime."

"Tell me the details and I'll do all I can", replied Sleuthman, trying to keep cool and ignore the pistol that the prospective client was holding under his raincoat.

"Will I be alive tomorrow?", he wondered.

Unit 5 /w/ wine /v/ vine

WHICH IS WORSE VERSE – WENDY'S VERSE OR WAYNE'S VERSE?

If you don't want to be misunderstood, then the answer lies in making a clear distinction between / v / and / w /:
verse *worse*

1. Listening: / w /

1.1 ***Which is the odd one out?***

a. b. c. d.

1.2 ***Which word(s) is / are correct?***

You will hear groups of words being spoken. Whenever you hear a / w / sound, tick the appropriate column.

	1.	2.	3.	4.
a. why b. queen c. wary d. whale e. rowing				

2. Articulation: / w /

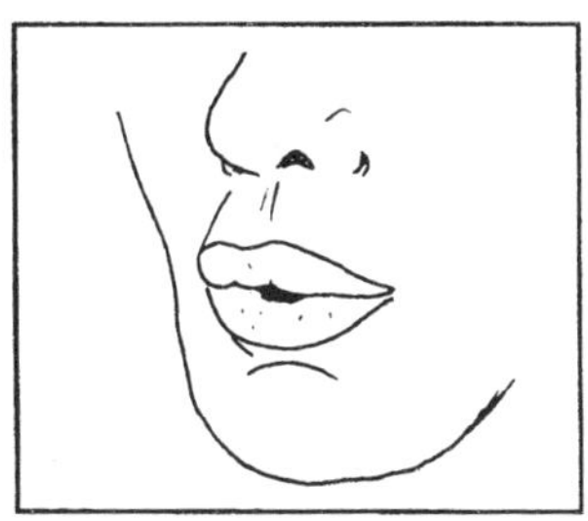

/ w /

Your lips should be rounded,
as in *sch**oo**l*.
Your lips mustn't touch your teeth.
Your lips mustn't vibrate
against each other.

Say ***wine***.

3. Listen and Speak

3.1	which	want	wasp	wood	what	weed
	twelve	twist	swim	swallow	queen	quick
	away	tower	rowing	lower	newer	lawnmower
	Wendy	Walter	William	Wayne	Howard	Dwight

N.B. **(i)** The /w/ sound at the end of the following words is only pronounced when the word coming after it begins with a vowel. Then the two words must be linked:

new - new‿armchair   row - row‿of houses

true - true‿answer   throw - throw‿away

(ii) In words ending in /ɔː/, the /w/ is never pronounced:

law raw saw

Remember that an intrusive /r/ is used to link words ending in /w/ with a vowel at the beginning of the next word. (cf. Unit 2, 1.2, p.32.)

4. Listening: /v/

4.1 ***Which is the odd one out?***

a. b. c. d.

4.2 ***Underline which of the following words you hear.***

1. van / fan	2. veal / wheel	3. vet / wet
4. vines / wines	5. leaf / leave	6. waif / waive
7. life / live	8. safe / save	9. first / worst / versed
10. fire / wire / via	11. file / while / vile	12. fail / veil / whale

5. Articulation: /v/

Place the upper teeth against the lower lip.
Don't say /f/ - you must add the voice!
Don't say /w/ - keep the upper lip still.
Vibrate the lips vvv-vigorously!
Say ***vine.***

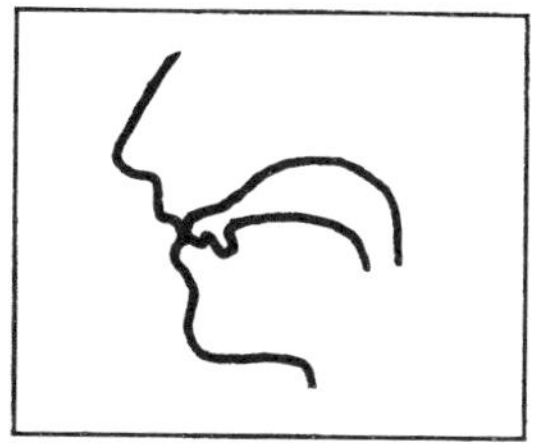

/v/

6. Listen and Speak

6.1

vase	vocabulary	very	visit	vain	voyage
over	hovercraft	level	cover	movie	never
drive	save	have	leave	move	cave

few - view	ferry - very	fat - vat	fan - van
wet - vet	wine - vine	while - vile	whale - veil

Vera, Veronica, Virginia, Vincent, Vanessa, Victor
Venice, Venezuela, Devon, Slovenia, Vienna, Liverpool

6.2 **Tongue Twister**

Which is worse verse - Wendy's verse or Wayne's verse?

6.3 **Sound differentiation – / r /, / w /, / v /, / f /:**

You must make clear differences between these sounds:

real / wheel / veal / feel
rail / whale / vale / fail
reign / wane / vain / feign

7. Dialogue: Gareth and Heather in Wilson's Wine Bar on Friday Evening

Gareth: Here's the glass of white wine you wanted.

Heather: Lovely. What's wrong with your leg?

Gareth: Er, I think I'm developing varicose veins.

Heather: How can you have varicose veins at your age? You ought to walk around and move about more.

Gareth: I know. Well, Wilson's Wine Bar isn't very lively even on Valentine's Day, is it?

Heather: No, but it's fine while we wait for your new woman to arrive.

Gareth: Vera Willows.

Heather: You ought to watch her - she's a positive devil. Given half a chance, she'll walk all over you.

Gareth: Anyone would think I was a real wimp.

Heather: Take my advice and leave that vamp of a woman well alone.

Gareth: But she's wonderfully creative and vivacious, and very lovely.

Heather: What about a really nice woman, like my friend Wendy Vanderbilt?

Gareth: But I want adventure, to live and love dangerously. Besides, what is there to prevent me from having my wicked way with a woman like Vera?

Heather: Varicose veins?

8.

Sing-a-long!

Listen to the /w/ sounds and the rhythm of this nursery rhyme.

The grand old Duke of York, he had ten thousand men,
He marched them up to the top of the hill,
And he marched them down again.
And when they were up, they were up,
And when they were down, they were down,
And when they were only half way up,
They were neither up nor down.

9. Word stress with suffixes

9.1 ***How is the stress pattern of the words below affected by adding suffixes? Listen to the cassette.***

mountain - mountaineer	license (vb.) - licensee	picture - picturesque
affect - affection	reflex - reflexive	climate - climatic
wonder - wonderful	comfort - comfortable	poison - poisonous

There are three categories:

1. *suffixes which are stressed*

ad**dress**	-	address**ee**	Ja**pan**	-	Japan**ese**
launder	-	launder**ette**	**stat**ue	-	statu**esque**
mountain	-	mountain**eer**	**en**ter	-	enter**tain**

2. *suffixes that change the stress to the last syllable in the stem:*

courage - cou**ra**geous	irony - **iro**nic
malice - ma**li**cious	mor**pho**logy - morpho**lo**gical
photograph - pho**to**graphy	**po**tent - po**ten**tial
generous -gene**ro**sity	
product - pro**duc**tive - produc**ti**vity	

3. *suffixes that do not change the stress placement:*

bear - **bear**able	**use** - **us**age	**cen**tre - **cen**tral
lead - **lead**en	**thought** - **thought**less	**bird** - **bird**-like
e**vent** - e**vent**ful	con**vince** - con**vinc**ingly	**mad** - **mad**ness
move - **move**ment	**moun**tain - **moun**tainous	**clock** - **clock**wise

9.2 ***Now apply the rules to the following words. Where is the primary stress? Say the words out loud.***

activity	artistic	authority	catlike
Chinese	comfortable	geographic	musical
production	refugee	successful	usherette

N.B. The stress rules of English are quite complicated and have been simplified here. There are also some exceptions:

to ad**mire**	-	**ad**mirable	ˈædmᵊrəbl
to pre**fer**	-	**pre**ferable	ˈprefrəbl

9.3 *Pronunciation of unusual suffixes*

English has a variety of uncommon suffixes which can cause problems.

suffix	pronunciation	examples
-ein(e)	iːn	caffeine, codeine, protein
-eity	ˈeɪəti (less often: ˈiːəti)	deity, spontaneity
-eur	ɜː	connoisseur, entrepreneur, poseur, voyeur. **But** when stress is on the first syllable, -eur becomes weak: amateur ˈæmətə, chauffeur ˈʃəʊfə
-gm	g is silent	paradigm ˈpærədaɪm, phlegm flem – **But** g is pronounced when between vowels: enigmatic ˌenɪgˈmætɪk, phlegmatic ˌflegˈmætɪk.
-ies	iːz	series, caries, rabies, species
-ile	aɪl	docile, fertile, virile ***But*** see p.10 for Am.E. versions

10. Exercises

10.1 ***Practise /w/ and /v/ sounds by repeating the dialogue, the Sleuthman text (ex. 10.10) and the listen and speak exercises.***

10.2 ***Where is the main stress in the following words? Practise saying them.***

adornment	allusion	ambiguity	assembly	assumption
attractive	circulate	department	education	footage
generosity	lengthwise	likewise	malicious	mountaineer
mountainous	poetic	preferable	productive	reduction
requirement	sensible	survival	sylphlike	tendency

10.3 ***Book titles: match the words to make famous book titles. Who wrote them? Then mark in the linking in these phrases, adding any extra sounds:***

Sons		The Fury
The Power		Mr. Hyde
Sense		Son
Crime		The Sea
Romeo		Peace
Dr. Jekyll	and	Lovers
The Old Man		Sensibility
War		The Glory
Dombey		Juliet
The Sound		Punishment

10.4 ***Put in the stress marks on these words. Check with your dictionary.***

volunteer - voluntary - voluntarily

photograph - photographer - photography - photographic

technique - technical - technology - technological - technician

character - characterise - characteristic - characteristically

person - personal - personality - personify - personification

economics - economic - economy - economical - economically

10.5 ***What possible suffixes could you put on the following words? Use your dictionary to help you. Can you then say them with the correct stresses? The first one is done for you.***

confiden(t) : **con**fidence **con**fidently confi**den**tial confi**den**tially

critic

effect

engine

enthus(e)

intellect

object

occup(y)

offic(e)

oppos(e)

politic(s)

possib(le)

pron(o)unce

provinc(e)

reliab(le)

sens(e)

theatr(e)

theor(y)

univers(e)

10.6 ***Can you say these words? Write them in phonetic transcription including stress marks, and check your answers in your dictionary.***

advantageous	interfere
amazing	mountainous
ascertain	punishment
biographic	reasonable
creative	tranquillity
employer	unique

10.7 ***How do we pronounce these places? Check in your English-English dictionary or a pronouncing dictionary for the transcriptions, then practise saying them. Pay particular attention to the <u>stresses</u> and the <u>weak forms</u>.***

Amazon
Arkansas
Asia
Athens
Berkshire
Berlin
Birmingham
Brussels
Calais
Cologne
Danube
Dublin
Durham
Edinburgh
Egypt
Eire
Folkestone
Florence
Ganges
Gloucester
Greenwich
Harwich
Heathrow
Illinois
Japan
Leicester
Mediterranean
Michigan
Missouri
Moselle
Naples
Niagara
Nile
Ostend
Paris
Portsmouth
Russia
Tennessee
Thames
Towcester
Vienna
Worcester

10.8 ***Can you read these sayings and who said them? Write them out in normal orthography.***

ˈməʊst ˈrɒk ˏʤɜːnəlɪzm | ɪz ˈpiːpl
hu kɑːnt ˏraɪt | ˈɪntəvjuːɪŋ ˈpiːpl hu
kɑːnt ˏtɔːk | fə ˈpiːpl hu kɑːnt ˎriːd   ˌfræŋk ˈzæpə

ˈevri dɪˈsɪʒn ju ˏmeɪk | ɪz ə mɪˎsteɪk   ˌedwəd ˈdɑːlbɜːg

10.9 Valentine's Day Messages.

Below are some examples of messages that people write in Valentine's Day cards. Read them out loud and compare your reading with the cassette. Write a short poem of your own that would be suitable for such a card.

Happy Valentine's Day

WILL YOU BE MY VALENTINE ?

Shall I compare thee to a summer's day?
Or perhaps a glass of Beaujolais?

Roses are red
Violets are blue
Sugar is sweet
And so are you

roses are red
violets are blue
my name is fred
and who are you?

r oses are red
v iolets are blue,
j ust to say
i still
love you.

10.10

SLEUTHMAN

Listen to the text about Sleuthman's holiday plans, paying particular attention to the /v/ and /w/ sounds, then read it aloud. Don't forget the linking!

In view of the very wet wintry weather of the previous four weeks, Sleuthman was feeling low on enthusiasm. He wondered whether to escape for a while to somewhere warmer. On Wednesday he had been reading about the wave of juvenile crime sweeping through Venezuelan villages. This fact had interested him for several reasons: Venezuela was warm, and would revitalise him after the ravages of an English November. He would be able to go in search of evidence for his book Victims of the World, and he could visit a very old friend of his, a Venezuelan violin virtuoso, who he had met in Wales when he had been investigating the vicious murders of five village workmen. All in all, Venezuela seemed like the perfect place to travel to, so, having made his decision, Sleuthman picked up the phone and booked a flight leaving at the weekend.

Unit 6 /ɪ/ bitter /e/ better /æ/ batter /ʌ/ butter

A BIT OF BUTTER MAKES BETTER BATTER

You will be misunderstood if you mix up these four sounds.

1. Listening

1.1 *Which is the odd one out?*

a. b. c. d.

1.2 *Which word(s) is / are correct?*

You will hear groups of words being spoken. Whenever you hear an /æ/ sound, tick the appropriate column.

	1.	2.	3.	4.
a. man b. sad c. can d. track e. mass				

2. Articulation: /e/ better /æ/ batter

Compare the following sounds:

/e/ Your mouth is slightly open and is stretched horizontally so that your laugh lines become noticeable, but not as wide as for /iː/ (see p.138). The front part of your tongue is raised.

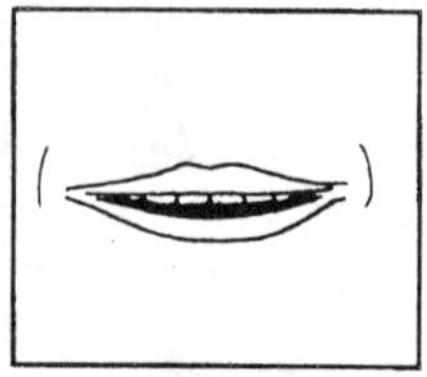

/e/

set

/æ/ Your mouth is stretched horizontally to the same degree as for /e/ but the most important point is that your mouth is ***wider open***. The front of your tongue is lower than for /e/. Be careful to say /æ/ , not /e/ ; are you saying ***sat*** or ***set***?

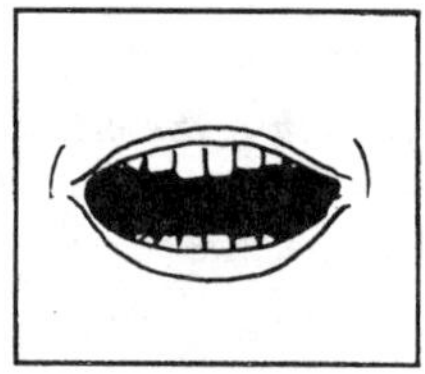

/æ/

sat

3. Listen and Speak

3.1

/e/:	set	pen	beg	head	mess	letter	pet	bet
/æ/:	sat	pan	bag	had	mass	latter	pat	bat

Note that both the above vowels are longer if the last consonant is voiced:

peck - peg   wet - wed   less - Les

lap - lab   sat - sad   match - Madge
rack - rag   bat - bad   back - bag

bad eggs   red ants   happy ending   black pepper
men's hands   pen pal   headband   camp beds

Andover	Blackpool	Canterbury	Halifax	Manchester
Atlanta	Alabama	California	San Francisco	Tallahassee
Mandy	Jack	Sally	Harry	Sam
Alison	Ann	Anthony	Daniel	Marion

4. Listening: /ʌ/ butter

4.1 *Which is the odd one out?*

a. b. c. d.

5. Articulation: /ʌ/

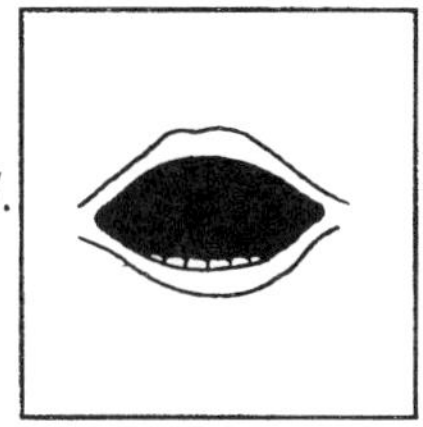

/ʌ/

The mouth is open a little ***more vertically*** than for /æ/ but you relax the muscles at the sides of your mouth so it is ***less spread horizontally*** than for /æ/. Stand in front of a mirror and say /æ/, then /ʌ/. Notice how your laugh lines are less prominent for /ʌ/.

Say **hut**.

6. Listen and speak

6.1

bat - but	cat - cut	fan - fun	swam - swum	began - begun
got - gut	fond - fund	boss - bus	wander - wonder	shone - shun
son	done	does	tongue onion	company
comfort	cousin	touch	worry oven	glove

7. Dialogue: Gareth's Bust-up

Heather: What's the matter, Gareth?
Gareth: Vera and I have just had a big bust-up.
Heather: Come, come, Gareth. Don't be sad -Vera's just having one of her mad tantrums.

Gareth: She called me a fat prat!
Heather: Forget her, Gareth. You can't marry that bag - she's a match for the devil, if ever I saw one!
Gareth: I've already packed my bags!
Heather: Come to my flat - it may not be a palace but it's grand enough for us. Let me pamper you.
Gareth: Er, thanks. But that'd be a bad plan.
Heather: I'd do it gladly for a fantastic man like you, Gareth.
Gareth: Oh, all right then. Thanks, Heather. Here, you carry my big black trunk and I'll just fetch my toothbrush.

8. Primary and secondary stress in polysyllabic words

So far we have looked at main-stressed and unstressed (/ə/) syllables. When the primary stress in longer words (four or more syllables) occurs late in the word, there is a secondary stress on the first or second syllable to indicate that this earlier syllable is not reduced:

Late stress + secondary stress:	sanitation	ˌsænɪˈteɪʃn
but	sabbatical	səˈbætɪkl

Say these words. Where are the primary and secondary stresses?

anniversary	European	definition
regeneration	pronunciation	apostrophe

9. More sentence stress

9.1 The most important factor in English intonation is the pitch of the highlighted syllable, <u>the tonic</u>: it may fall or rise.

It's raining (falling) = statement
It's raining? (rising) = question

A shift in the tonic can change the meaning:

The *dog* didn't bite the postman.	(Perhaps the cat did!)
The dog didn't *bite* the postman.	(It barked at the postman.)
The dog didn't bite the *postman.*	(It bit the neighbour.)
The dog *didn't* bite the postman.	(You've misunderstood the story.)

9.2 Listening

Use a highlighter pen to pick out the accented word.

1. I thought you said Mary was coming tonight.
2. You shouldn't have gone to so much trouble.
3. Are these the keys you've been looking for?
4. Did Henry VIII want to get rid of all of his wives?

10. Exercises

10.1 ***Practise speaking the dialogue and the listen and speak exercises until the /e/ and /æ/ sounds are near-perfect!***

10.2 ***Mark the primary and secondary stressed syllables in the following words. Practise saying them and check yourself by listening to the cassette.***

academic	anthropology	articulate (adj.)	colloquial
conservative	correspondent	dissertation	hydroelectric
inexplicable	international	irritable	methodological
microscopic	obligatory	onomatopoeia	opposition
philharmonic	population	postgraduate	propaganda
protagonist	punctuation	responsibility	theoretical

10.3 ***Practise changing the highlighted word yourself, as in 9.1. Do you know what you are indicating in each case?***

1. My husband doesn't walk like a rhinoceros.
2. I don't think he loves you.

10.4 ***How do we say these names? Listen to the cassette and then repeat.***

Barbara Cartland	Somerset Maugham	Edgar Wallace
Samuel Pepys	William Faulkner	Keats
D.H. Lawrence	Lewis Carroll	Guinness
Sherlock Holmes	Agatha Christie	John Le Carré

10.5 ***Who are these authors? Practise saying the names out loud.***

ˌwɪljəm ˈʃeɪkspɪə	ˌʤɔːʤ ˈɔːwel	ˌʤeɪn ˈɒstɪn
ˌwɪljəm ˈwɜːdzwəθ	ˌfeɪ ˈweldən	ˌiː em ˈfɔːstə
ˌʃɑːlət ˈbrɒnti	ˌʤɔːʤ ˈeljət	ˌʤeɪmz ˈʤɔɪs
ˌtɒməs ˈhɑːdi	ˌʤɒn ˈfaʊlz	vəˌʤɪniə ˈwʊlf

10.6 Abbreviations

What is an acronym? Which of these are acronyms? Can you say them? What do they stand for?

Educational Qualifications

MD	PhD	MA	MSc
BA	BSc	GCSE	

Writing and Research

e.g.	i.e.	cf.	viz.
et al.	ibid.	N.B.	PTO

Politics and International Institutions

PM	MP	MEP	UN
NATO	UNESCO	UNICEF	

Weights and Measures

lb.	oz.	in.	mph

10.7 Idioms Time!

Here are some idiomatic expressions in phonetic script with no gaps, as they would often be spoken in natural conversation (i.e. using contractions, reductions and weak forms.) Practise saying them aloud. Check in your dictionary if you don't know all the meanings.

1. ɪtˈkeɪmaʊtəvðəˎbluː
2. hizˈfʊləvˎbiːnz
3. aɪvgɒtˈpɪnznˎniːdlz
4. aɪˈhævntgɒtəˎkluː
5. juvˈbɪnnɪpˎtɒf
6. aɪdəvbɪnəzˈsɪkəzəˎpærət
7. hikənˈiːtlaɪkəˎhɔːs
8. judəvˈʤʌmtaʊtəvjɔːˎskɪn

Unit 7 /s/ ice /z/ eyes

I ONLY HAVE ICE FOR YOU!

1. Listening

1.1 *Which is the odd one out?*

a. b. c. d.

1.2 *Underline the word you hear on the cassette, a or b.*

a.	police	loose	lice	hearse	race	docks	rips	pats
b.	please	lose	lies	hers	rays	dogs	ribs	pads

2. Articulation of /z/ eyes

The tongue rests lightly against the alveolar ridge. While vibrating your vocal cords, you form a narrow valley in the front part of your tongue. Air then escapes along this valley. N.B. - a vowel before /z/ is usually longer than before /s/:

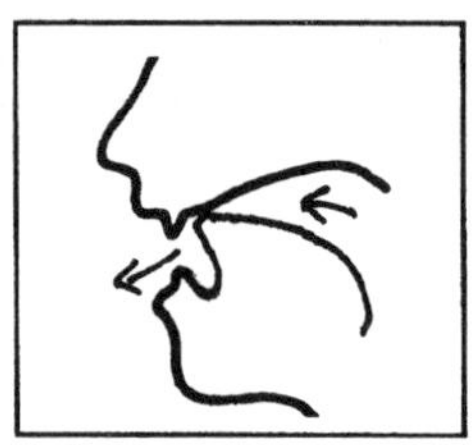

tongue position for /s/ and /z/

ice - eyes

Say /z/ at the end of words after voiced consonants (e.g. beans /bi:nz/) but /s/ in all of the following:

pencil pulse pence false insect else incense

3. /s/ or /z/? A few guidelines

It is not always easy to know whether to use /s/ or /z/, but here are a few rules to help you. Remember, there are exceptions.

/s/

- in words beginning with 's': *sentence, song*
- for most words with double 'ss': *fussy, classy, glass, rissole* (but /ʃ/ *for '–ssion'* and *'–ssur–': session, discussion; pressure, pressurise, fissure, assurance* – see also p.121.)
- for the letter 'c' when it precedes 'e' and 'i': *police, celebration, decide, ice, pencil, receive*
- before voiceless consonants: *school, special, skip, sphere*
- in plurals where '–s' follows a voiceless consonant: *hats, sacks, cups, lips*
- in possessive forms after voiceless consonants: *Keith's, Pat's, Beth's*

/z/

- for the letter 'z': *zoo, dizzy, sizzle*
- for '–ss–' in *scissors*
- for the third person singular ending of many verbs: *is, was, does, has, goes, sees, lies, etc.*
- after voiced consonants, e.g. *woods, eagles, pens, bags*
- in most plurals ending in '–s' (except after voiceless consonants): *bombs, turkeys, dominoes, crises, curfews*
- in possessive forms after vowels or voiced consonants: *Joe's, Mary's, John's, Susan's*

4. Listen and Speak

4.1

zip	zero	zulu	zebra	zoom
cosy	wizard	busy	dizzy	transient

/s/	peace	pace	police	close *(adj.)*	lace	racks	mops	writes	use *(nn.)*
/z/	peas	pays	please	close *(vb.)*	lays	rags	mobs	rides	use *(vb.)*

Desmond	Giles	Leslie	Miles	Elizabeth	Rosemary	Susan
Bahamas	Brazil	Israel	Philippines	Venezuela	Zambia	Wales

N.B. 1. house /haʊs/ ***but*** houses /ˈhaʊzɪz/

2. The genitive of names ending in /s/ takes a /z/:
Alice /ˈælɪs/ ***but*** Alice's /ˈælɪsɪz/

3. In a few words, an initial 'x' is pronounced /z/:
Xerox /ˈzɪərɒks/ xylophone /ˈzaɪləfəʊn/ xenophobic /ˌzenəˈfəʊbɪk/

4.2 Tongue Twisters

Underline the /z/ sounds. Can you say these phrases quickly?

Suzie's scissors *Suzie's scissors* *Suzie's scissors*

sizzling sausages *sizzling sausages* *sizzling sausages*

5. Intonation when giving information or instructions

5.1 Falling Tones:

As previously mentioned, the tones of English utterances are generally falling at the end. We use falling tones when we want to imply that we've finished speaking, for example when giving information or instructions and when introducing a new topic or new information. Listen to these examples on the cassette.

1. giving information:

The Police Station is in Prince's Street.
Our semester begins on the seventh of April.
The time is now five past seven.
Mr Greaves isn't here; he's away on business.

2. giving instructions:

Turn right at the next crossroads.
Give me two loaves of granary, please.
Fido, come here!
Children, go and play outside!

3. new topic information:

I'm at the police station.
I was arrested.
I've just bought a new car.
It's my birthday tomorrow.

6. Dialogue: Gareth phones Heather from the police station

Gareth: Hello, is that you, Heather?
Heather: Gareth, your voice is strange, as if you've been crying.
Gareth: I'm at the police station. They're accusing me of stealing diamonds from the jeweller's.
Heather: That's ridiculous. It sounds like a pack of lies to me.
Gareth: Of course it is.
Heather: Some police officers are over-zealous, I realise that, but there must be a reason for their suspicions.

Gareth: I presume their decision is based on my similarity to James the Gemsnatcher. You know, the one who's been on the news.

Heather: Oh, yes. Yes, there is a resemblance. But he's got brown eyes and takes size seven shoes.

Gareth: Minor details like that are lost on the police. Please call my solicitor, Mr. Jones. He'll advise me. I don't want to spend years in the cells.

Heather: You don't want to pay his exorbitant bills. You know I'm an expert on television courtroom dramas, Gareth. You're safe in my hands.

Gareth : Er, on second thoughts, prison doesn't sound so bad.

7. Listen and speak

Mark in the intonation patterns. Then repeat the phrases, imitating the intonation patterns carefully:

Come here!	He's next door.	Go and find it!
It's down the road.	Put it over there.	I'm too busy now.
I agree entirely.	I'm going on Monday.	She's on holiday.

8. Exercises

8.1 ***Repeat the dialogue and listen and speak exercises until the /s/ and /z/ sounds are near-perfect!***

8.2 ***Which is correct - /s/ or /z/ ?***

Say the plural forms of the following nouns:

road	mat	chair	house	dock	tube
crash	theme	eye	rose	watch	louse

Say the third person singular form of the following verbs:

look	go	run	sit	love	help
read	fill	say	choose	catch	lose

Say the possessive forms of these names:

John	Judith	Edward	Graham	Joyce
Mary	Vince	James	Alice	Frank

8.3 ***What instructions or directions would you give in the following situations? Remember to use falling intonation at the end. The first one is done for you.***

Situation		Instruction
It's cold in here.	➔	*Close the window, please.*
The children are making a noise.	➔	
You ask the way to the train station.	➔	
You're feeling thirsty.	➔	

8.4 ***Read the following text.***

/ˈsluːθmæn ˈɡəʊz tə ðə ˎzuː/

ɪt wəz ˎθɜːzdeɪ | ən ˈsluːθmæn dɪˈsaɪdɪd tə ˈvɪzɪt ðə ˎzuː

hiː həd ˈhɜːd ðət ɪt wəz ˈpɒsəbl tə ˈlɜːn əbaʊt ˈhjuːmən bɪˏheɪvjə |

baɪ əbˈzɜːvɪŋ ði ˎænɪməlz

hɪz ˈfɜːs ˏstɒp | wəz ðə ˎmʌŋki ˌhaʊs

ɡəˈrɪləz rɪˈzembl əs ˇməʊst | hi ˏriːznd | bət ˈɑːftər ə ˈfjuː ˏmɪnɪts |

hi ˌsɔː ˈnʌθɪŋ ðət wʊd ˈhelp wɪð ɪz ˎwɜːk | səʊ i ˈmuːvd ˎɒn.

ˈweə dɪd i ˈɡəʊ ˎnekst | ənd ˎwaɪ ?

ˈraɪt jɔːr ˈɑːnsə ˎhɪər | ɪn fəˈnetɪk ˎskrɪpt - ˈfɪfti ˎwɜːdz ˌpliːz

....

....

....

....

....

8.5 ***Listen to the recipe being described on the cassette. Can you guess what is being cooked? Notice the intonation patterns used by the speaker.***

8.6 Recipes

(a) ***Describe a recipe in English to someone you know. Don't choose something too easy! Start by giving the ingredients and then describe the method. Your friend has to guess what the recipe is for. Try to concentrate on falling tones at the end of statements and instructions.***

(b) ***Write down in phonetic script the main ingredients of the following two items:***

(i) moussaka	*(ii) your favourite savoury dish*
....	....
....	....
....	....
....	....
....	....
....	....

8.7 Words ending in '---man'

Names, professions and various other titles ending in '---man' have two pronunciations: some are pronounced with the strong form / mæn / and others have the weak form / mən /. Sort the following list into two columns according to pronunciation:

postman	Superman	milkman	dustman
Batman	bogeyman	Sleuthman	strongman
fisherman	barman	walkman	doorman
workman	clergyman	boatman	horseman
spaceman	fireman	seaman	gentleman
Englishman	Scotsman	Welshman	Irishman

/ æ /	/ə /

8.8 More abbreviations

Time

BC	AD	am	pm	asap

Defence

NASA*	CIA	CID	FBI	RAF	HMS

Computers

BASIC*	DOS*	http	RAM*
www	WYSIWYG*	PC	

Miscellaneous

GP	JP	VIP	RSVP	UFO**
SOS	AIDS*	BBC	ITV	RIP
VAT**	DIY	YUPPIE*	DINKY*	NIMBY*

... and a couple of very modern ones:

MINT* LOMBARD*

* These are always read as acronyms, i.e. you pronounce them as whole words without naming the individual letters.

** These can be pronounced either as acronyms or by saying the individual letters.

Unit 8 /ʊ/ good /uː/ food /ɜː/ served

GOOD FOOT SERVED HERE !

1. Listening

1.1 ***Which of the following sounds is being spoken? Write down the number of the sound:***

1. /uː/ as in *food*
2. /ʊ/: as in *foot*

a. b. c. d. e. f. g. h. i. j.

1.2 ***Write out the words you hear in normal orthography.***

a. b. c. d. e.

2. Articulation of /u:/ food

The English /uː/ is not a pure vowel sound but slightly diphthongised: /ə/+/uː/, as in *move*. Begin with the lips in a neutral position /ə/, then round your lips and push them forward to form /uː/. The lip position is the same as for /w/ , as at the beginning of *wet*.

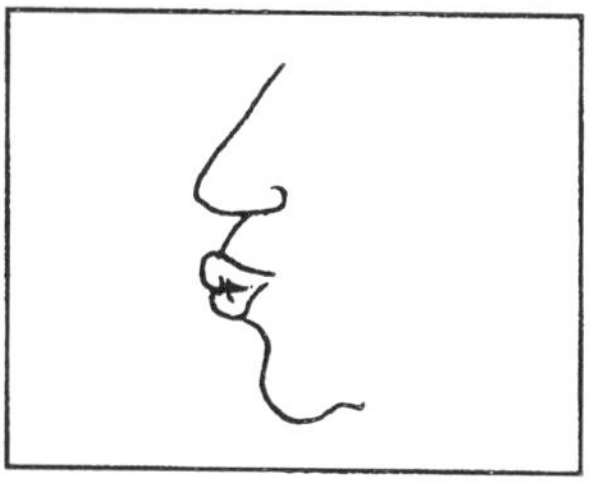

/u:/

/uː/ is slightly longer before voiced consonants, as in *food* and shorter before voiceless consonants, as in *fruit*.

Try not to get it mixed up with the short sound /ʊ/, as in *foot*.

N.B. In some forms of *Northern English* , /ʊ/ is pronounced /uː/: book /buːk/; cook /kuːk/

3. Listen and Speak

3.1

food	shrewd	lose	soothe	prove	who'd	
boot	shoot	loose	tooth	proof	hoot	
foot	soot	look	took	put	hood	
Lucy	Ruth	Julie	Trudy	Bruce	Hugh	Jude

3.2

Limerick

There was a young vicar from Bude
Who liked to cook Indian food.
At Mass he served curry,
They left in a hurry,
Which put him in quite a bad mood.

4. Articulation of /ɜː/ verse

Lips should be neutral and only very slightly apart. The whole mouth is relaxed. Say "earl".
/ɜː/ is the long form of /ə/.
In Br.E. (unlike Am.E.), don't say an /r/ after /ɜː/ as in *heard, third, absurd*. Especially after /w/ concentrate on unrounding your lips for the /ɜː/ sound:

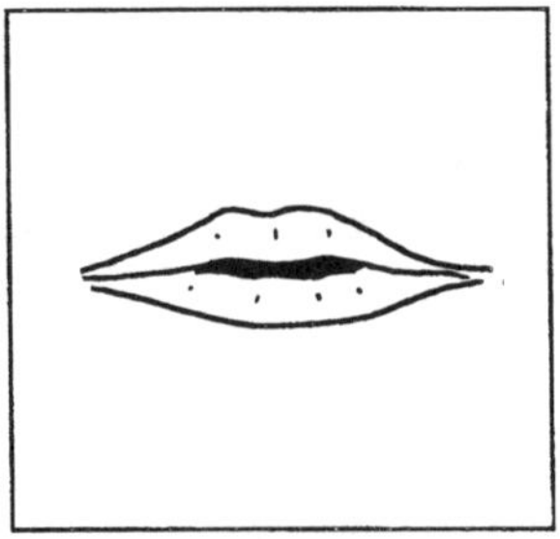

/ɜː/

word   world   worse   work   were

5. Spelling

5.1 ***There are several ways of spelling /ɜː/:***

<u>ear</u>l	h<u>er</u>	wh<u>ir</u>l	w<u>or</u>k	c<u>ur</u>l

How do you spell the words you hear on the cassette?

a. b. c. d. e. f.

6. Listen and speak

6.1

earl	fern	hurl	pearl	worm
learner	murder	turner	fur	girl
Bert	Bernard	Fergus	Shirley	Earnest

6.2 **Tongue Twister**

Were her first words German words or Turkish words?

7. Intonation

Intonation - rising tones

The main uses of rising tones are:

- to speak about old or shared information;
- to show we want confirmation or further discussion;
- to give a soft command or to show politeness.

7.1 Giving old / shared information

Listen and repeat:

Fergus: You know that autobiography you were telling me about?
Shirley: Yes, do you want to read it?
Fergus: Yes, I'd like to.
Shirley: I think it's on the top shelf.

7.2 Wanting confirmation or further discussion

Listen and repeat:

Fergus: So you enjoyed reading the book?
Shirley: Well, most of it. It was entertaining, as biographies go.
Fergus: I'll take it with me, O.K.?
Shirley: Sure. Will you return it before I move away?

7.3 Giving soft commands, showing politeness

Listen and repeat:

Fergus: Well, have a nice time in Wales.
Shirley: Thanks. When are you going on holiday?
Fergus: Not sure. I'll probably stay at home.
Shirley: Oh, don't do that. You need a break.

N.B. The more words there are after the tonic, the more slowly the voice rises.

Listen and repeat:

You know that autobiography?
You know that autobiography you were telling me about?
You know that autobiography you were telling me about last week?

7.4 Intonation in Questions

Here we shall practise three types of question formation:

(1) **Yes / No questions** - questions needing a "Yes" or "No" answer;

(2) **"Wh– " questions** - questions which begin with a "Wh–" question word or with "How";

(3) **Alternative questions** - questions which give a choice.

(1) Yes / No questions

These mostly have a rising intonation at the end. Listen and repeat:

Is it raining at the moment?
Are you feeling all right?
Is the shop closed?
Are you still living in London?

N.B.: A falling intonation is also possible in such questions, but less common, e.g. if we highlight a certain word before the end because we are surprised:

Are you still living in London?
Is it raining at the moment?

(2) "Wh– questions"

These mostly have a falling intonation. Listen and repeat:

Where's the key?
When did you post the letter?
Why did you do that?
How will you get there?

N.B.: A rising intonation is possible in such questions, but less common, e.g. if we highlight a certain word at the end:

Where's the key?
Why did you do that?

(3) Alternative questions

Here we notice a rising intonation on the first alternative and falling intonation on the second. Listen and repeat:

Do you prefer red wine or white wine?
Is Sofia the capital of Bulgaria or Romania?
Are you coming to visit on Monday or Tuesday?
Does Lucy come from Plymouth or Exeter?

N.B. ***As we have already seen on rising intonation, the more words there are after the tonic, the more slowly the voice rises. Listen and repeat:***

Did you see Edward?
Did you see Edward last night?
Did you see Edward at the party last night?

8. Dialogue: The virtues of shirts, shoes and burgers

Heather: That's the worst purple shirt I've ever seen.
Gareth: How rude of you!
Heather: And your new blue shoes are too crude for words.
Gareth: Phew! You are in a gruesome mood. Would a burger improve your humour?
Heather: Yes, but I'd prefer not to return to Trudy's Fast Food: it's rather dirty and there are too few seats.
Gareth: True, and the girl who works there on Thursdays always burns the burgers.
Heather: Have you heard about Percy's? They serve good food and it doesn't cost the earth.
Gareth: Ah yes, the third turning past the Turkish Tearooms. Now, would you like their superb bird's nest soup or turtle dove stew?
Heather: Er, burnt burgers sounds perfect.

9. Exercises

9.1 ***Repeat the dialogue and listen and speak exercises until you're near-perfect!***

9.2 ***You are the head of a firm. One of your secretaries, Bert, is often late for work. This morning, at 9.05, you burst into the office to question Trudy, the other secretary. What would you say under the circumstances? Write possible questions or statements in the gaps, and then practise speaking the dialogue, paying attention to your intonation.***

You:
Trudy: No, I haven't seen him this morning.
You:
Trudy: I've got no idea.
You:
Trudy: I don't think that's fair.
You:
Trudy: Yes, you're right.
You:
Trudy: Yes, I think so.
You:
Trudy: If you like.
You:
Trudy: I could be here by eight o'clock.
You:
Trudy: Thank you.
You:
Trudy: O.K., I will.

9.3 ***Match the two halves of the sayings. Practise saying them.***

Music soothes	first served.
The proof of the pudding	favours the brave.
No news	the savage breast.
Fortune	deserves another.
A bird in the hand	is good news.
First come,	is in the eating.
One good turn	is worth two in the bush.

9.4 *Sounds crossword*

Write the phonetic transcription of the words in the clues. Diphthongs count as one sound.

Clues across

1. A comfortable seat wide enough for two or three people.
3. The opposite of beautiful.
6. The Biblical character who built The Ark.
7. An interjection expressing sudden pain.
8. To bend the upper part of the body forward as a way of showing respect.
9. Adjective meaning terrible, serious.
10. A man's name, very popular among kings of England.
11. A preposition.
13. To express a wish that great misfortune will happen, usually by calling on magical powers.
14. The part of the face in which the teeth are set.
15. A present form of the verb to be.
16. An adjective meaning complete, total; a verb meaning to speak (sometimes with difficulty)
18. Opposite of wetly.

Clues down

1. Two pieces of bread, usually with butter and some other filling between them (pl).
2. Prettily coloured plants. You buy them in bunches.
3. To take one's clothes off.
4. A verb meaning to move or travel.
5. A place for conducting experiments.
10. Possessive form of she.
12. Another verb for to chew or bite, mostly for animals when they're eating something hard, e.g. bones.
13. Another word for murdered.
17. To let out a deep breath slowly, usually to express sadness, tiredness or pleasure.

9.5 Dictation exercise

SLEUTHMAN

Listen to the cassette to fill in the missing parts of the text.

Sleuthman couldn't keep up with ____________________________

____________________________but he did notice a slip of paper

falling to the pavement.____________________________

____________________________. Through one of his unofficial liaisons, he

managed____________________________. He kept watch

on the block of flats, hoping to catch sight of the boy________________

____________________________. "Got you!" screamed Sleuthman.

____________________________.

"Well, you shouldn't keep your cheques________________________."

9.6 ***Sort the following into two columns according to vowel quality.***

mood	soup	crook	hood	rue	strewn	wool
crew	cue	prune	shook	soot	fluke	wood

/uː/	/ʊ/

9.7 ***Write the phonetic symbol of the vowels or diphthongs in each word:***

heard	word	yearn	
heart	fear	tear	or
shirt	wear	ear	
shears	sword	early	

9.8 ***Transcription from phonetics into traditional orthography***

As we have seen, there are various spellings for the sounds /uː/, /ʊ/ and /ɜː/. Write out all possible versions of the following words in traditional orthography.

fuːl	ruːt	pɜːl	luːs
nɜːs	luːz	suːt	ʤuːs
wʊd	kɜːlz	θɜːd	tɜːf
buːð	mɜːdə	muːs	sɜːli

Unit 9 /-b/ /-p/; /-d/ /-t/; /-k/ /-g/; /-f/ /-v/

HAND BACK MY HANDBAG!

What's the English for:

- the opposite of good – *bat* or *bad*?
- the place the British like to go for a drink in the evening – *pup* or *pub*?
- the thing you carry your shopping in – *back* or *bag*?
- a broadcast on TV that you're watching as it's happening – *life* or *live*?

1. Listening: underline the one you hear, a. or b.

a.	lap	pick	life	hat	back	rip	proof	clock
b.	lab	pig	live	had	bag	rib	prove	clog

2. Articulation: /b/ /d/ /g/ /v/

Make sure you use your voice for all these sounds.

/b/ Both lips touch together lightly.

/d/ The tongue touches lightly against the upper alveolar ridge.

/g/ The back of the tongue touches lightly against the soft palate.

/v/ The upper teeth rest on the lower lip with a lot of vibration.

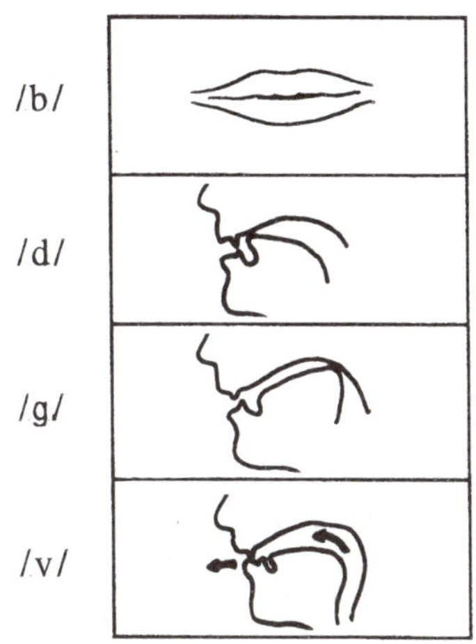

It may help at first to add a small extra /ə/ sound after the consonant if you find these sounds difficult:

lab /læbə/ head /hedə/ pig /pɪgə/ live (adj.) /laɪvə/

3. Listen and Speak

3.1 ***Say the following, making the differences clear.***

slap - slab	mat - mad	peck - peg	life - live (adj.)
set - said	rack - rag	safe - save	dock - dog
wick - wig	bit - bid	bat - bad	leaf - leave

bad egg	red robe	language lab	wave a hand	old rags
a hard jog	wide road	wild hive	good cards	five knives

3.2 ***Listen and repeat this well-known rhyme:***

Monday's child is fair of face,
Tuesday's child is full of grace,
Wednesday's child is full of woe,
Thursday's child has far to go,
Friday's child is loving and giving,
Saturday's child works hard for its living,
And a child that's born on the Sabbath day,
Is fair and wise and good and gay.

N.B. There are many possible pronunciations of *Wednesday,* the most common of which are 'wenzdi and 'wenzdeɪ ; (less often) 'wednzdeɪ, 'wednzdi.

'Gay' here has the original meaning of 'happy', 'cheerful', and not 'homosexual'.

4. Syllabic Consonants: /dn/ garden /tn/ beaten

The consonant /n/ in final position after /d/ and /t/ can be pronounced either with a schwa sound /ə/ or as a syllabic consonant /n/. Thus *garden* can be /ˈgɑːdən/ or /ˈgɑːdn/. (cf. Syllabic consonants, **Unit 4, 6, p.53.**)

With the syllabic /n/ the air is passed out through the nasal passages. Remember, this form is *more common in natural, spoken English.* This phenomenon also often occurs when /n/ follows a consonant in combinations: *good night, kidney, at night.*

But in standard British English the final /n/ is <u>not</u> syllabic when there is an /n/ before the /d/ or /t/. Thus *London* is /'lʌndən/ <u>not</u> /'lʌndn/.
cf: *mountain, sentence.*

4.1 ***Listening: Which do you hear, syllabic /n/ or /ən/?***

pardon forgotten written Britain beaten

4.2 ***Listen and Speak:***

/n/: wooden garden rotten pardon suddenly hidden Britain
/ən/: wooden garden rotten pardon suddenly hidden Britain
/n/: The wooden button was hidden in the garden.
/ən/: The wooden button was hidden in the garden.

5. Intonation in Echo Questions

5.1 An echo question is a response which normally has one of two functions:

(a) it asks for more information;
(b) it shows surprise.

An echo question finishes with a high rising intonation.

5.2 ***Listen***

(a) asking for more information:

Babs: My husband's just had a breakdown.
Bob: A breakdown? Is he in hospital?
Babs: No, he's on the M25.
Bob: The M25?
Babs: Yes, he's waiting for the AA. (= Automobile Association)

(b) showing surprise:

Greg: You know that poetry competition? I won first prize.
Jill: You won a prize?
Greg: Yes, a trip for two trekking at the North Pole.
Jill: The North Pole?
Greg: Yes, I've told them you'd come with me.

5.3 Listen and Speak

Listen to the dialogues in 5.2 again and repeat, paying particular attention to the intonation.

5.4 Intonation in echo responses of agreement and disagreement

We often react to statements with short responses of agreement or disagreement.

Listen to the examples on the cassette and notice the highlighted syllables, then try to copy the intonation.

A: I live in London.	B: So do I! C: I don't. I live in Bristol.
A: I'm a student.	B: So am I! C: I'm not. I work in a bank.

6. Tongue Twisters

Gavin is a crooked cricket critic.

Kay gazed back at Pamela Catchpole's black bag.

Dopy Peter dropped his tepid pot of tea onto Danny's toe.

7. Dialogue: Gareth gives up his job.

Gareth: I've just given up my drab dead-end job at the college.
Heather: Your job?
Gareth: Yes, my job. I'd like to rove around the wide world before I'm too old.
Heather: Rove around? That sounds like a bad idea.
Gareth: A bad idea? But life is a sad, hard drag. I couldn't stand living if things didn't improve.
Heather: A sad, hard drag? Who planted that odd view of life in your head?
Gareth: I thought you were supposed to be my friend. Nobody understands me.
Heather: Don't they? I find your mind as complicated as an amoeba.
Gareth: Complicated? You do? I didn't know you cared.
Heather: Let's go to the pub and I can delve into that addled mind of yours.
Gareth: Addled?* You're a friend indeed. By the way, what *is* an amoeba?

**Addled* = when the brain is confused.

8. Exercises

8.1 ***Practise the final /b/ /d/ /g/ /v/ sounds in the words and dialogues in this unit by listening to the cassette and speaking the exercises out loud.***

8.2 ***Practise the syllabic /n̩/ sound by speaking the examples.***

8.3 ***Practise the intonation in echo questions by listening to the cassette and repeating.***

8.4 ***Complete the following dialogue, beginning with an echo question every time.***

A: Guess what! I've just bumped into Bob.

B:

A: Yes, he's just got back from Baghdad.

B:

A: He was helping to build a gigantic dam.

B:

A: No, that was his last job, the one in the Punjab.

B:

A: No, he was definitely in India.

Now practise speaking the dialogue with the correct intonation.

8.5 ***Make up a conversation as in examples (i) and (ii) below, based on the words given. Then try to copy the intonation of the speakers on the cassette who are reading the following two examples:***

Person A:	**Person B:**
(i) *London*	*Paris*
I went to London last week.	London? I thought you were going to Paris.
(ii) *Uncle Tom / at the weekend*	*Auntie Jean*
I'm visiting Uncle Tom at the weekend.	Uncle Tom? I thought you were going to visit Auntie Jean.
1. *cinema*	*theatre*
2. *steak and chips / supper*	*pizza*
3. *TV / after lunch*	*gardening*
4. *music*	*fill in your tax form*
5. *pub / Friday evening*	*visit me*

8.6 ***Practise echo responses of agreement and disagreement by reacting to the following (see 5.4):***

1. I can play the guitar.
2. I like English pop music.
3. I work as a waitress.
4. I prefer the theatre to the cinema.
5. I drive a Ford.

8.7 ***Avoiding potential misunderstandings***

If you said the underlined words wrongly what might be understood?

The lioness has given birth to three <u>cubs</u>.

I can't walk in these <u>clogs</u>.

What a <u>wide</u> river!

She wore an evening <u>robe</u>.

He said <u>he'd</u> wave.

Let's go for a <u>ride</u> in the country.

You have a lovely crocodile-skin <u>bag</u>.

I'd like a <u>crab</u> sandwich, please.

He promised to <u>wed</u> me.

Make sure you understand both words.

8.8 **Joke Time!**

1. ˈwɒt dɪd ðə ˈsiː ˌseɪ tə ðə ˎbiːʧ?
   ˎnʌθɪŋ | ɪt ˈʤʌst ˎweɪvd!

2. wɒts ˈblæk ən ˏwaɪt |
   ən ˈred ɔːl ˎəʊvə?
   ə ˎnjuːzpeɪpə

3. ˌrəud ˎseɪfti ˌnəutɪs | 'autsaɪd ə ˎskuːlː
'draɪv ˎkeəfli | 'dəunt 'kɪl ə ˎʧaɪld |
'weɪt fər ə ˎtiːʧə

4. 'waɪ dəz ði 'əuʃn ˎrɔː?
ˎwel | 'wudn ˋʧuː | ɪf ju haed ˏkraebz ɒn jɔː ˌbɒtəm?

5. 'waɪ kaːnʧu 'staːv ət ðə ˎsiːsaɪd?
bɪˌkəzəv ðə ˎsaendwɪʧɪz ˌðeə!

8.9 ***Write out a joke or an amusing short story in phonetic transcription.***

....

....

....

....

....

....

....

8.10 ***Vowel + gh: arrange the following in the columns shown according to pronunciation. Then check your answers in the key.***

although	rough	bough	ought	trough
borough	cough	bought	dough	fought
enough	through	brought	thorough	drought
tough	sought	nought	though	plough

/əʊ/	/ʌf/	/aʊ/	/ɔː/	/ə/	/ɒf/	/uː/

Unit 10 /b– / /p– / /d– / /t– / /k– / /g– / /f– / /v– /

HAVE YOU PIN TO CRATE PRITAIN?

1. Do you often travel by drain?
Do you wear classes?
Have you seen the changing of the carts?
Let's all bray* for peace.
She bought a four-wheel-drive VW fan.

*bray = to make the sound that a donkey makes

As you can see, making mistakes with voiced and voiceless consonants can lead to amusing and embarrassing misunderstandings!

2. Listening

2.1 ***Underline the one you hear:***

bin - pin   dent - tent   girl - curl   bear - pear   dear - tear   gold - cold

2.2 ***Which is the odd one out?***

a.   b.   c.   d.

3. Articulation: /p/ /b/; /t/ /d/; /k/ /g/ before vowels

Voiceless /p/, /t/, /k/ should be aspirated strongly.
The sounds /b/, /d/ and /g/ should be pronounced much more softly, with little or no aspiration, and using the voice.
(For articulation diagrams, see Unit 9, p. 99)

You can check yourself by holding the palm of your hand up ten centimetres in front of your mouth. With the aspirated voiceless sounds, you will feel the air on your palm. You should feel almost nothing when you say the voiced sounds.

You can also practise saying the sounds near a lighted candle. The aspirated voiceless sounds will blow out the candle, whereas the voiced sounds should not. Don't burn your lips!

/p/ /b/

4. Listen and Speak

4.1

bee	-	pea	bit	-	pit	bush	-	push
bobby	-	poppy	double	-	couple	symbol	-	simple
dense	-	tense	dime	-	time	down	-	town
ladder	-	latter	rider	-	writer	medal	-	metal
gum	-	come	goat	-	coat	guard	-	card
bigger	-	bicker	anger	-	anchor	angle	-	ankle
van	-	fan	very	-	ferry	view	-	few

4.2 **Tongue Twister**

Peter Piper picked a peck of pickled pepper,
A peck of pickled pepper Peter Piper picked,
If Peter Piper picked a peck of pickled pepper,
Where's the peck of pickled pepper Peter Piper picked?

5. Listening: /bl/ /pl/ /br/ /pr/ /gl/ /kl/ /gr/ /kr/ /dr/ /tr/

5.1 *Underline the one you hear:*

black	-	plaque	great	-	crate	drain	-	train
glass	-	class	brawn	-	prawn	drew	-	true

5.2 *Which is the odd one out?*

a. b. c. d.

6. Articulation: /bl/, /br/, /dr/, /gl/, /gr/

Make sure you aren't saying /pl/, /pr/, /tr/, /kl/, /kr/!
Make light touches of your tongue, lips etc., and use your voice throughout both sounds.

6.1 *Listen and Speak:*

/bl/:	blank	-	plank	blot	-	plot	bleed	-	plead
/br/:	breast	-	pressed	brick	-	prick	bride	-	pride
/dr/:	drain	-	train	dry	-	try	drew	-	true
/gl/:	glass	-	class	glad	-	clad	glue	-	clue
/gr/:	grain	-	crane	great	-	crate	grew	-	crew

Bridget, Brian, Graham, Greg, Sandra, Adrian, Andrew

6.2 Joke Time !

Question 1: 'wɒts ˏgreɪ | ˌhæz 'fɔː ˏlegz | ənd ə ˎtrʌŋk?

Question 2: 'wɒts ˏbraʊn | ˌhæz 'fɔː ˏlegz | ənd ə ˎtrʌŋk?

Question 3: ɪf ə 'red 'haʊs ɪz 'meɪd əv ˏred ˌbrɪks |
ənd ə 'bluː 'haʊs ɪz 'meɪd əv ˏbluː ˌbrɪks |
wɒts ə ˎgriːn ˌhaʊs meɪd ɒv?

Answers:

1. ə 'maʊs 'gəʊɪŋ ɒn ˎhɒlədeɪ
2. ə 'maʊs 'kʌmɪŋ ˎbæk frəm ˌhɒlədeɪ
3. ˎglɑːs

7. Assimilation

7.1 Unpronounced Plosives

What's the difference? – big eight - big gate

To make the sounds /b/, /p/, /d/, /t/, /g/, /k/ we normally release air in a sudden exp<u>los</u>ion (hence "<u>plos</u>ives"). When two of these sounds occur together the final consonant of the first word and the first consonant of the second word are pronounced together as a slightly longer consonant. Notice it is the *second* plosive that is "exploded".

7.2 *Listen and Speak: underline the one you hear:*

red eye - red dye	bright eyes - bright ties	her bread - herb bread
top layer - top player	black ape - black cape	big oats - big goats

You will have noticed that the first plosive is not pronounced fully. This often happens in normal, spoken English. Now listen again and repeat.

7.3 ***Notice the same thing happens even when the plosive consonants are different:***

/d/	→ /b/	goo(d) boy
/d/	→ /k/	goo(d) coffee
/t/	→ /p/	tha(t) play
/t/	→ /ʤ/	grea(t) joke

7.4 ***When /ʤ/ and /ʧ/ occur together, both plosives are pronounced:***

orange jumper	'ɒrɪnʤ 'ʤʌmpə	Which chair?	'wɪʧ 'ʧeə
orange chair	'ɒrɪnʤ 'ʧeə	Which jumper?	'wɪʧ 'ʤʌmpə

7.5 ***Notice how /n/ becomes /ŋ/ before /g/ or /k/ in the following examples:***

we can go   in case   increase   ten cups   fine grain

7.6 ***Cross out the unpronounced letters and practise speaking:***

a. She was wearing a deep purple dress.
b. They had dinner at nine o'clock.
c. We've got a flat tyre, I'm afraid.
d. She gave him a big kiss.
e. What are my job prospects after the course?
f. I bought a large chest of drawers.
g. The next section's about tag questions!
h. I waited for ten more minutes.
i. My teacher said I've got good pronunciation.

8. Intonation in Tag Questions

There are two main intonation patterns for tag questions:

8.1 • Falling intonation if you aren't expecting a response. In most cases there is also a fall on the last word before the falling tag:

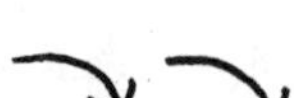

Ghosts don't exist, do they?

8.2 • Rising intonation if you want confirmation. (Intonation of the part before the tag depends very much on which word(s) is / are stressed.)

You don't believe in ghosts, do you?

8.3 ***Listen and mark the intonation of the question tag: is it going up or down? Check your answers in the key, then listen again and copy the intonation. For each sentence, try to think what situation could cause the speaker to use the intonation given on the tape.***

1. She is going to marry him, isn't she?
2. You will come for dinner, won't you?
3. You're not going to let him treat you like that, are you?
4. They're not arriving today, are they?
5. It's not true, is it?
6. You still love me, don't you?
7. You are taking your medicine, aren't you?
8. You have paid, haven't you?
9. John won't go, will he?
10. You won't lose it, will you?

8.4 Positive tag questions after positive statements

These are most commonly used in polite conversation to show interest in what the speaker is saying. Similarly, when you are expressing surprise or if there is an element of challenge, sarcasm or even disdain in your response, the following pattern is used, with falling intonation before the tag and rising intonation on the tag:

Oh, you're vegetarian, are you?
We're having beef, are we?
Oh, you've come after all, have you?
You want to see him again, do you?

Note that this type of question tag sentence, with no 'not', accounts for **around 40%** of all sentences containing a question tag.

8.5 Answering question-tag questions

Situation:	A single English businesswoman meets a German businessman (who is also single, though she doesn't know it) at a party in London. After a few minutes of conversation, she asks him something.
Question:	You aren't married, are you?
Wrong answer:	Yes (that's right).
Correct answer:	No (I'm not married).

This can lead to misunderstandings! When answering, think of the correctness of the situation, ("No, I'm not married") not of the sentence ("Yes, what you are saying is correct.").

To make things clear, it often helps to add a phrase like, "No, I'm not" or "Yes, I am". If you *do* put several words in your anwer like this, there is a different intonation pattern according to whether you are agreeing or disagreeing with the first speaker. In examples (1) and (2) below, speaker A in both cases has a **falling** intonation on the question tag. Look what happens with speaker B's intonation in the replies:

(1) A: English is a terribly difficult language, isn't it?

B: Yes, it is. (**falling** when **agreeing** with A)

(2) A: English is a terribly difficult language, isn't it?

B: No, it isn't! (**rising** - at least at the end - when **disagreeing** with A)

Listen to these questions and the way they are answered, and repeat them, paying attention to your intonation:

1. You aren't English, are you?
2. English grammar isn't easy, is it?
3. English pronunciation isn't very difficult, is it?
4. Most students don't like doing tests, do they?
5. You couldn't swim across the Atlantic, could you?

9. Dialogue: Gareth and Heather discuss trains, cars and a friend's brother.

Heather: You know Vera's brother, don't you?
Gareth: What, Brian the train driver from down town?
Heather: Precisely. He's a great bloke, isn't he?
Gareth: He's crazy. You know he believes that big vehicles should be banned from Great Britain, don't you?
Heather: Yes, it's a brilliant plan, isn't it? He has a truly terrific brain, and noble principles. I really admire him.
Gareth: Brian? But he's got bad breath, greasy hair and a dreadful glassy gleam in his eyes.
Heather: No he hasn't. By the way, I think he quite fancies me.
Gareth: But his clothes are all grimy and grey from driving his trains all day.
Heather: Trust you to drag dress into the argument. Appearances don't count in my book.
Gareth: Well, I'm flabbergasted. To think you'd fall for a dreary eco-freak when there's a dynamic, bronzed Greek God right here.
Heather: Bronzed?

10. Exercises

10.1 ***Listen to the cassette and repeat the dialogue and listen and speak exercises for the* /b/, /d/, /g/, /bl/, /br/, /gl/, /gr/ *and* /dr/ *sounds until you are near-perfect.***

10.2 ***Match up an adjective from list A with a noun from list B below. What different pairs can you make? Practise saying the words, concentrating on the plosive sounds.***

A: black - bad - great - smart - lead - good - wide - big - red

B: time - gap - pipe - table - dog - gate - cow - baby - job

10.3 ***Complete the sayings and practise saying them:***

It's like trying to get ______ out of a stone.

_______ minds think alike.

_______ is thicker than water.

You can lead a horse to water, but you can't make him ______

10.4 ***Write five facts about Great Britain which you're fairly sure of and five facts you're not at all sure of. End each one with a question tag. Mark the intonation, and practise asking your questions and answers.***

Five facts you're fairly sure of.

e.g. The Prime Minister works in London, doesn't he?

____ ?

____ ?

____ ?

____ ?

____ ?

Five facts you're not at all sure of.

e.g. The British national dish is fish and chips, isn't it ?

____ ?

____ ?

____ ?

____ ?

____ ?

10.5

SLEUTHMAN

Below is a story about one of Sleuthman's adventures. Unfortunately it is all mixed up. Can you put the sentences into the correct order? Then read the correct version onto a cassette.

a. "I'm glad I've been going to the keep-fit class," muttered Sleuthman under his breath as he swiftly jumped over the four-foot railing.

b. "That was a good night's work," he chuckled as he stole quietly out of the garden.

c. "My client won't have to worry any more about being blackmailed."

d. "Now, where would Doug Ugger hide papers?"

e. "I'm in luck," he whispered to himself as he found that the French window was unlocked.

f. Deftly he flicked open the little hinged door and took out the photos.

g. He flattened himself against the house wall and stayed in the shadow.

h. "Yup, these are the negatives."

i. He let himself in.

j. "They're all the same, these crooks, no respect for religion," he thought, as he detected the secret compartment in the statue of Jesus.

Correct sequence: ....

10.6 ***Can you read these sayings and who said them? Do you agree with them?***

1. ˈsaednɪs ˈəʊnli ˎmʌltɪplaɪz ɪtˌself. |
ˈlet ʌs ˈduː aʊə ˏdjuːti | əm bi ˎʧɪəfl.

ˈsaemjuəl ˈʤɒnsən

2. ˈkləʊðz ˈmeɪk ðə ˎmaen. | ˈneɪkɪd ˏpiːpl
haev ˈlɪtl ɔː ˈnəʊ ˈɪnfluəns ɒn səˎsaɪəti.

ˌmɑːk ˈtweɪn

3. tə bi ˈrɪəli mediˇiːvl | wʌn ʃʊd haev ˈnəʊ ˎbɒdi
tə bi ˈrɪəli ˇmɒdn | wʌn ʃʊd haev ˈnəʊ ˎsəʊl
tə bi ˈrɪəli ˇgriːk | wʌn ʃʊd haev ˈnəʊ ˎkləʊðz

ˌɒskə ˈwaɪld

Unit 11 /ʧ/ cheeses /ʤ/ Jesus

I LOVE CHEESES – HALLELUJAH!

1. Listening

For each pair, underline the word you hear:

a.	chop	job	b.	choke	joke
c.	rich	ridge	d.	besiege	beseech

2. Articulation of /ʧ/ and /ʤ/

The major difference in the articulation of /ʧ/ and /ʤ/ is that the latter should be voiced in most positions:

voiceless:	/ʧ/	=	/t/ + /ʃ/	
	cheeses		choke	chin
voiced:	/ʤ/	=	/d/ + /ʒ/	
	Jesus		joke	gin

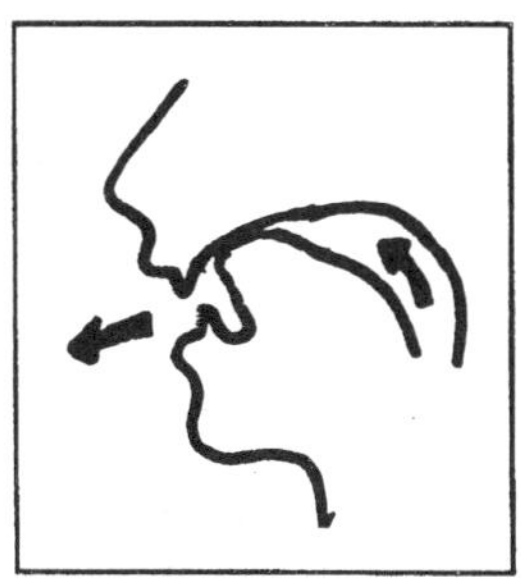

/ʧ/ and /ʤ/

N.B.: An initial 'g' is usually pronounced /ʤ/ before 'y':

gym, gyrate .... and generally before the letters 'e' and 'i':
gel, genetic, gin, gist.
Main exception: gynaecology ˌgaɪnəˈkɒləʤi

3. Listen and Speak

3.1

a. giant cheeseburger
b. Norwegian engineer
c. Jumbo jet
d. ginger fudge
e. orange jelly
f. digital television
g. cheap jewellery
h. Sergeant Major
i. German sausage
j. logical decision

3.2 rich - ridge match - Madge wretch - Reg batch - badge

wedge hedge huge large seige rage porridge sage village
Bridget Geraldine Jackie Jean Roger Gerald Geoff

nature mixture lecture literature
adjective adjust soldier danger

N.B.: /d/ and /t/ can change to /ʤ/ and /ʧ/ when followed by /j/ (assimilation):

would you? /ʤ/ could you? /ʤ/ let yourself go /ʧ/

3.3 Tongue Twisters

Jews choose Chinese juice.

John chose a giant cheeseburger.

Imagine an imaginary menagerie manager managing an imaginary menagerie!

4. Listening: /ʃ/ nation /ʒ/ occasion

4.1 ***Listen to the following words, each of which contains either a /ʃ/ or a /ʒ/ sound. Write the relevant symbol after each word.***

leisure	issue	rouge	station	measure
television	decision	relation	usual	dishes

5. Articulation of /ʒ/: leisure

5.1 This sound is articulated like /ʃ/ but must be voiced!

cash	-	casual	fission	-	vision
mesh	-	measure	pressure	-	pleasure
leash	-	lesion	session	-	seizure
flesh	-	leisure	trash	-	treasure

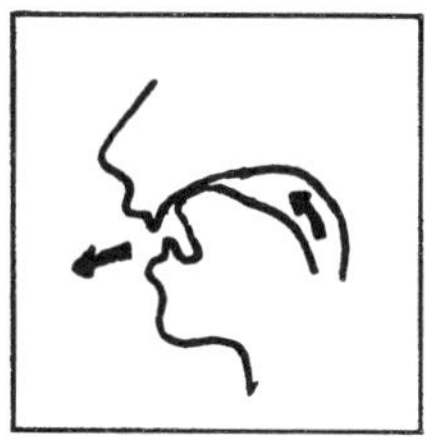

/ʒ/

N.B. The sound /ʒ/ rarely occurs in initial position, and then only in loan words, e.g. genre /ˈʒɒnrə/ (French)

5.2 ***Listen and Speak:***

measure	decision	casual	confusion	usual	revision
prestige	rouge	beige	massage	montage	garage*

* This word has several other acceptable pronunciations in Br.E. The next two most common are: /ˈgærɑːʤ/ and /ˈgærɪʤ/.

6. Dialogue: The pleasures of English cuisine

Heather: What's that strange smell wafting out of the kitchen?
Gareth: Oh, I've just been putting the finishing touches to a delicious surprise for you.
Heather: You shouldn't have gone to so much trouble, Gareth.
Gareth: It's my speciality: tangerine jelly and chocolate Angel Delight*, sausage rolls and cheddar cheese sandwiches.
Heather: That doesn't sound very nutritious.
Gareth: The occasional indulgence in stodgy food is perfectly natural, I assure you.
Heather: Yes, but too much cheap junk food can endanger your health.
Gareth: Oh, you just think we should all eat that vegetarian rubbish you enjoy so much.
Heather: Such old-fashioned prejudices are unusual in someone of your age.
Gareth: You just don't appreciate English cuisine, that's all.
Heather: Actually, I'm allergic to English food.
Gareth: But it's your heritage!
Heather: You can enjoy two portions, then. I'm meeting Roger and John for sushi at that new Japanese restaurant in Regent Street.
Gareth: Wait for me!

*Angel Delight, as the name suggests, is a deliciously light concoction, available in a packet and rich in chemical flavours. Just add milk and whip, and the result is a dessert bearing a faint resemblance to genuine *blancmange* blə'mɒnd*ʒ*.

7. Stress in Place Names

7.1 In place names we stress the last word, except in combinations containing the word *street:*

Central **Park** Abbey **Road** Waterloo **Station** *but* **Regent** Street

Connect the following, then practise saying them with the correct intonation.

Regent's	Square
Heathrow	Palace
Buckingham	Abbey
Westminster	Crescent
Oxford	Airport
Windermere	Street
Leicester	Park

8. Leaving out sounds

There are various situations when sounds are sometimes left out in natural, spoken English. (See syllabic consonants, Unit 4, p.53 and Unit 9, p.100; assimilation in unpronounced plosives, Unit 9, p.111.) Here are some more examples of this phenomenon:

8.1 Elision

French	frentʃ	becomes	frenʃ	punch	pʌntʃ	→	pʌnʃ
lounge	laʊndʒ	→	laʊnʒ	orange	'ɒrɪndʒ	→	'ɒrɪnʒ
mostly	'məʊstli	→	'məʊsli	firstly	'fɜːstli	→	'fɜːsli
tasteful	'teɪstfl/	→	'teɪsfl	textbook	'tekstbʊk	→	'teksbʊk

8.2 Compression This occurs where two syllables are compressed into one:

convenient	kən ˈviːniənt	-	kən ˈviːnjənt
rattling	ˈrætəlɪŋ	-	ˈrætlɪŋ
normally	ˈnɔːməli	-	ˈnɔːmli
particularly	pəˈtɪkjələli	-	pəˈtɪkjəli and pəˈtɪkli
potato	pə ˈteɪtəʊ	-	pˈteɪtəʊ
police	pəˈliːs	-	pliːs

9. Exercises

9.1 ***Practise speaking the dialogue and listen and speak exercises until the /ʤ/ and /ʧ/ sounds are near-perfect.***

9.2 ***Finish these place names – say them with the correct stress!***

Windsor......................	Madison Square*......................	Covent ....
Speakers'	The Brandenburg	Princes ....
Pall	Victoria	The Rocky ....
Trafalgar	Winchester	Wall ....
Sydney	Long	Downing ....
Piccadilly......................	Mexico......................................	The .... Mahal
The .... Lakes	Horseguards...............................	
The Eiffel	.... Gate Bridge	

*The rule for stress in place names with three or four words is the same as for those with two words, i.e. it is **the last word** which takes the main stress:

Hyde **Park**

Hyde Park **Corner**

The Old Kent **Road**

9.3 ***Imagine (maybe you don't need to!) that you are so starving that you dive into the nearest McJunkald's fast food restaurant. You want a complicated mixture on your hamburger or sandwich, and a milk shake, but what mixture and what flavour? Complete the dialogue.***

Assistant: What can I get you?

You: ____

Assistant: What would you like on it?

You: ____

Assistant: Sauce?

You: ____

Assistant: Do you want chips with this concoction?

You: ____

Assistant: Something to drink?

You: ____

Assistant: What flavour? We have 32 mouth-watering temptations.

You: ____

Assistant: That'll be £12.30.

You: ____

9.4

SLEUTHMAN

Follow the text about Sleuthman as you listen to it on the cassette. Where two or three alternatives are given, underline the word you hear. Then practise speaking the text yourself, paying particular attention to voiced and voiceless sounds:

The calm before the storm: Sleuthman is seen here looking forward to an apéritif. Twenty minutes later he was having problems with a chunk of meat!

Sleuthman was *joking / choking* when he said he didn't want the *chop / shop / job*. It was all *Chas's / Jaz's / Shaz's* fault for patting him on the back just as he was about to swallow. For a moment he couldn't breathe, but then he lifted his *gin / shin / chin*, swallowed, and felt much better. "Of course I want it," he said, secretly thinking what a *sure / chore / jaw* it all sounded. Then he began shovelling pieces of meat into his mouth. His friend had just offered him the chance to *shop / chop / job* an old enemy, Mr. *Edge / Etch / Eshe*, known for the carved initials he left at the scene of each successfully accomplished crime. "I'll begin right away."

Just as he was about to ask for the bill, Sleuthman remembered he only had small change in his jacket pocket. "Er, *Chas / Shaz / Jaz*," he asked, "could I *catch / cash / cadge* a fiver off you? I'll pay you back tomorrow. Honest."

9.5

fəˈnetɪk ˌsaʊndz ˌpʌzl

All the clues refer to food and drink.

1.					ʧ				
2.	ʃ						■	■	■
3.			ʃ					■	■
4.					ʤ	■	■	■	■
5.	ʧ						■	■	■
6.							ʒ	■	■
7.	ʤ			■	■	■	■	■	■
8.			ʤ					■	■
9.	ʃ				■	■	■	■	■
10.						ʤ	■	■	■
11.	ʤ			■	■	■	■	■	■

Clues

1. In British English these are called chips (two words).
2. This drink is popular for big celebrations.
3. These can be collected in the woods, but be careful not to pick the wrong ones!
4. A Scottish breakfast speciality.
5. People can become addicted to this delicious, sweet brown treat.
6. A dessert made with milk; it comes in different flavours.
   Clue: Gareth uses a packet version.
7. An alcoholic drink often mixed with tonic.
8. A widely used substitute for butter.
9. An apéritif from Spain.
10. A healthy green vegetable: Popeye's favourite!
11. A fruity spread for toast.

5.4 Stress pattern and meaning

Notice how the difference in meaning is reflected in the stress pattern:

a black **board** - a board that is black.
blackboard - a board for writing on in the classroom.

a **black**board   a black **board**

6. Exercises

6.1 ***Practise the dialogue and the listen and speak exercises, paying particular attention to the diphthongs.***

6.2 ***Write a short poem using as many of the following words as possible. Use a dictionary to help you if necessary. Practise reciting your poem.***

gold	day	break	beard	fear
sight	boys	old	town	mine
snow	die	smoke	how	noise
stay	about	make	low	hair

9.5

fəˈnetɪk ˌsaʊndz ˌpʌzl

All the clues refer to food and drink.

1.					tʃ				
2.	ʃ						■	■	■
3.			ʃ					■	■
4.					dʒ	■	■	■	■
5.	tʃ						■	■	■
6.							ʒ	■	■
7.	dʒ			■	■	■	■	■	■
8.			dʒ					■	■
9.	ʃ				■	■	■	■	■
10.						dʒ	■	■	■
11.	dʒ			■	■	■	■	■	■

Clues

1. In British English these are called chips (two words).
2. This drink is popular for big celebrations.
3. These can be collected in the woods, but be careful not to pick the wrong ones!
4. A Scottish breakfast speciality.
5. People can become addicted to this delicious, sweet brown treat.
6. A dessert made with milk; it comes in different flavours. Clue: Gareth uses a packet version.
7. An alcoholic drink often mixed with tonic.
8. A widely used substitute for butter.
9. An apéritif from Spain.
10. A healthy green vegetable: Popeye's favourite!
11. A fruity spread for toast.

Unit 12 Diphthongs: /eɪ/ /ɪə/ /eə/ /ʊə/ /aɪ/ /ɔɪ/ /əʊ/ /aʊ/

SEE YOU LATER, ALLIGATOR! IN A WHILE, CROCODILE!

English has several diphthongised vowels where some other languages (as well as some regional varieties of Enghlish) use purer forms, e.g. ray so loud.

1. Listening

1.1 ***Which do you hear: a diphthong (as in Standard Southern British English) or a purer vowel (as in Standard Northern British English)? Underline where you hear a diphthong.***

bate	bay	raid	taker	made	mail
day	lake	rain	place	way	May

2. Articulation of /eɪ/:

The mouth must be relaxed. The first sound is like /e/ in *bed*. This sound - like all diphthongs - is a gentle glide from one sound to another. The mouth closes slightly for the second part, the tongue moves up a bit and the lips spread slightly. All movements are relatively small.

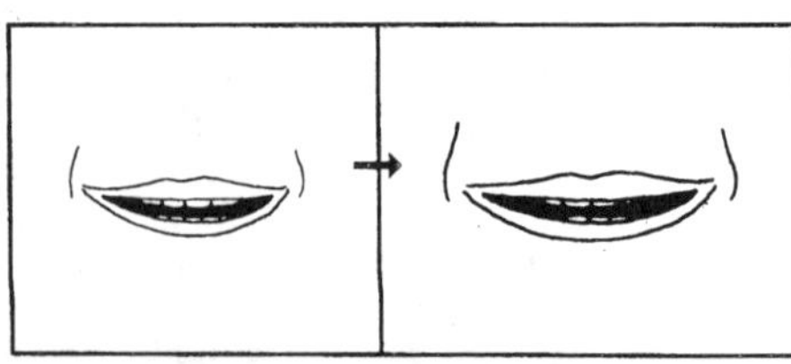

3. Listen and Speak:

3.1 *Before voiced consonants /eɪ/ is longer:*

place - plays	mate - made	state - stayed	safe - save
wait - wade	paint - pained	late - laid	h - age

Ada	Daisy	Elaine	Grace	Hazel	Jane
Adrian	David	Ray	Craig	Jason	Wayne

3.2 Other Diphthongs: /ɪə/ /eə/ /ʊə/ /aɪ/ /ɔɪ/ /əʊ/ /aʊ/

/ɪə/ As with /eɪ/, the mouth is relaxed. The two sounds of the diphthong flow smoothly into one another:
here weird beer fierce we're

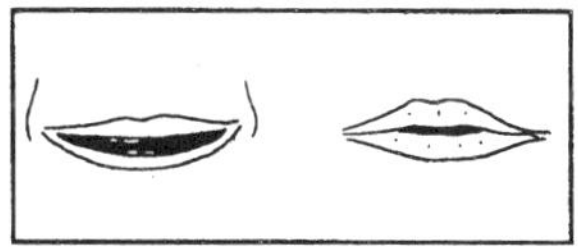

/eə/: Begin with /e/, as in *bed*:
air parents pear hair tear wear

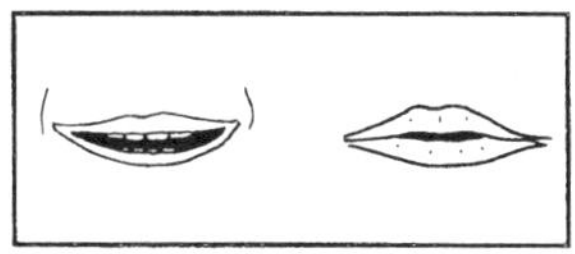

/ʊə/: The lips are less rounded than for /uː/, more relaxed:
cure pure lure endure manure

N.B: words like *sure tour poor* are now more commonly pronounced
/ʃɔː/ /tɔː/ /pɔː/

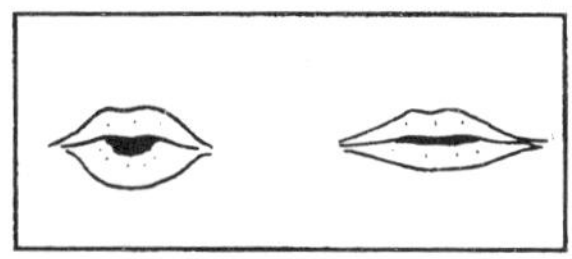

/aɪ/: high night buy try mile

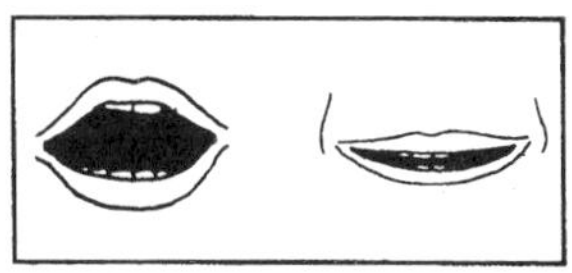

/ɔɪ/: noise boy oil enjoy boiled

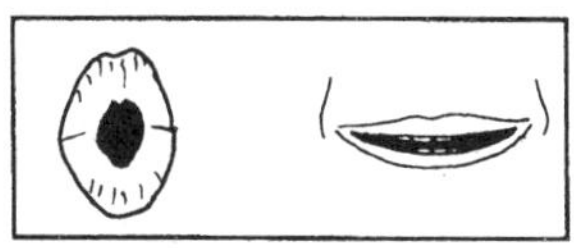

/əʊ/: home rope so only code
(This sound shifts towards /ɒʊ/ when an 'l' follows, e.g. *old, coal, fold.*)

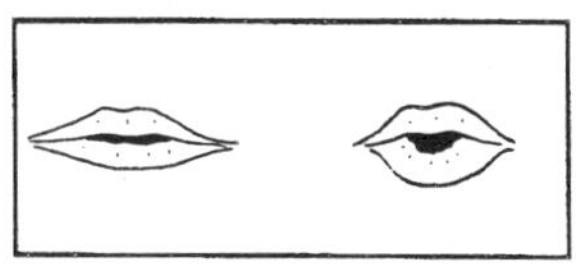

/aʊ/: town loud how frown bound

4. Dialogue: At night in the Underground Station

Heather: Did you hear that weird noise?
Gareth: Where? Outside on the stairs?
Heather: I'm not sure. It sounded like a howling bear.
Gareth: Look, there are no bears in South Croydon.
Heather: I'm aware of that. Let's take the next train home. I'm so cold and I'm wary of this neighbourhood.
Gareth: But it's only nine o'clock, and we've decided to have an exciting night in town.
Heather: We might die in an odious crime.
Gareth: You amaze me with your crazy fears. Why don't we go to the Rock 'n' Roll café in Highgate?
Heather: That awful dive? All they do there is meet their rowdy mates, drink loads of beer, play the machines and rave all night to noisy techno sounds.
Gareth: Exactly.

5. Stress in Compound Words

5.1 Why is it possible to say "**English** teacher" and "English **teacher**"?*

Where is the main stress in the following compounds?

Christmas cake	writing pad	flying saucer
car ferry	inner city	roof rack
gingerbread	glass bowl	gripping film
walking stick	mineral water	bookcase
good-looking	ginger beer	teapot

As you can see, the situation is rather complicated. However, below there are some guidelines to help you.

* The meaning changes depending on what is stressed:

an **English** teacher - a teacher of English (here *English* is a noun)
an English **teacher** - a teacher who is English (here *English* is an adjective)

Guidelines:

5.2 • **Early Stress**

1. When the two parts of the compound are written as one word:

   gingerbread **book**case **tea**pot **fruit**cake

2. When the two parts are both nouns:

   roof rack **car** ferry **tape** recorder

3. Where the first part of the compound ends in *–ing* and is used as a noun (gerund). The '--ing' part then normally tells you the *function or use* of the second word.

   writing pad (a pad that is used for writing)
   (A writing **pad** would be a pad that writes!)

   walking stick (a stick that is used for walking)
   (What would a walking **stick** be?)

4. When the second part of the compound is *cake, juice or water:*

   Christmas cake **mineral** water **orange** juice

5.3 • **Late Stress**

1. In compounds which are written either hyphenated or as two words, and where the first word is an adjective or an adverb:

   good-**looking** inner **city**

2. Where the first part of the compound ends in -ing, and is the present participle form, used as an adjective or a verb:

   gripping **film** flying **saucer**

3. Where the first word is the name of the material or the ingredient:

   ginger **beer** glass **bowl**

5.4 Stress pattern and meaning

Notice how the difference in meaning is reflected in the stress pattern:

a black **board** - a board that is black.
blackboard - a board for writing on in the classroom.

a **black**board

a black **board**

6. Exercises

6.1 ***Practise the dialogue and the listen and speak exercises, paying particular attention to the diphthongs.***

6.2 ***Write a short poem using as many of the following words as possible. Use a dictionary to help you if necessary. Practise reciting your poem.***

gold	day	break	beard	fear
sight	boys	old	town	mine
snow	die	smoke	how	noise
stay	about	make	low	hair

6.3 ***Put the following words into the correct column according to their vowel sounds. Check any words you are not sure of in your dictionary. Practise saying each column out loud.***

brooch	mauve	beige	heir	rein	tied	fear	slain
convey	sigh	pear	spear	foe	sleight	snail	rye
queer	veil	oats	prey	sew	alloy	toil	rowdy

/eɪ/	/eə/	/aɪ/	/ɔɪ/	/əʊ/	/aʊ/	/ɪə/

6.4 ***Mark the primary stress in the following compounds:***

travel agent's	pepper pot	semi-detached	bookshop
saltcellar	ham sandwich	semicircle	well-educated
lemon juice	blackbird	rocking horse	outboard motor
front door	bathwater	washing powder	paper towel
first class	turning point	pot-bellied	flowerpot
well-fed	narrow-minded	dishwasher	living room
apple tree	apple pie	cherry brandy	cherry pip
plum pudding	plum tree	tomato soup	tomato plant
beef crisis	beef stew	fish knife	fish fingers
cheesecake	spring water	grapefruit juice	milk pudding
History teacher	central heating	mobile phone	ponytail
dinner-jacket	water bottle	fruitcake	cleaning-lady

6.5 ***Use a highlighter pen to mark the main stress in the following words. Explain their meanings, making the differences clear:***

a wet suit
a wetsuit

an Italian teacher
an Italian teacher

a driving lesson
a driving ambition

a white house
The White House

a running machine
a running machine

a travelling salesman
a travelling bag

a flying club
a flying saucer

a rolling stone
a rolling pin

6.6 ***Make up some compounds using words from lines A and B. Highlight the primary stresses.***

The first one has been done for you: ill-ad**vised**

A	**B**
ill-	box
land-	sauce
hotel	house
chatter-	Charles
hand-	moon
cheese	writing
broken-	satisfied
honey-	lady
Prince	hearted
Central	jam
ground	cleaner
green-	floor
vacuum	porter
blackcurrant	Station
self-	***advised***

6.7 ***Below is a poem illustrating some of the difficulties of English spelling. Can you find the missing words from the list below and put them in the correct gaps? The rhymes (aa bb) should help you!***

bed	**great**	**suite**	**bird**	**dough**
sword	**mother**	**debt**	**bear**	**through**

Pronunciation Traps

I take it you already know
Of tough and bough and cough and_______________.
Others may stumble, but not you,
On hiccough, thorough, laugh and________________.
Well done! And now you wish, perhaps,
To learn of less familiar traps.
Beware of heard, a dreadful word
That looks like beard and sounds like_______________.
And dead: it's said like______________, not bead,
For goodness sake, don't call it 'deed.'
Watch out for meat and__________________ and threat
(They rhyme with_________ and straight and_________.)
A moth is not a moth in_________________.
Nor both in bother, broth in brother.
And here is not a match for there,
Nor dear and fear for________________ and pear.
And then there's dose and rose and lose -
Just look them up - and goose and choose,
And cork and work and card and ward,
And font and front and word and_______________,
And do and go and thwart and cart.
Come come, I've hardly made a start.
A dreadful language? Man alive,
I'd mastered it when I was five!

6.8 ***How many words can you make by adding a phonemic vowel in the following? Use your dictionary to check your creations!***

Example:

/p___t/:	/pɪt/ pit	/pæt/: pat	/pet/: pet	/pɒt/: pot
	/piːt/: peat	/pʊt/: put	/pɔːt/: port	/pɜːt/: pert etc.

1. /k__p/
2. /l__n/
3. /b__d/
4. /gr__m/
5. /fl__t/

6.9 ***Can you read these sayings and who said them? Do you agree with them?***

1. ˌedjuˈkeɪʃn həz prəˌdjuːst ə ˈvɑːst ˌpɒpjəˈleɪʃn ˈeɪbl tə ˎriːd | bət ˇʌneɪbl tə dɪˌstɪŋgwɪʃ | ˌwɒt ɪz ˌwɜːθ ˎriːdɪŋ.

   ˌʤiː ˌem trəˈveljən

2. ˌtelɪˈvɪʒn ɪz ən ɪnˇvenʃn | ðət pəˈmɪts ju tə bi entəˈteɪnd ɪn jɔː ˇlɪvɪŋ ˌruːm | baɪ ˈpiːpl ju wʊdnt ˈhaev ɪn jɔː ˎhəʊm.

   ˌdeɪvɪd ˈfrɒst

3. ˈɔːl ˈwɪmɪn bɪˈkʌm laɪk ðeə ˎmʌðəz – | ˈðaet ɪz ðeə ˈtræʤədi.
   ˈnəʊ ˎmaen ˌdʌz – | ˈðaets ˎhɪz.

   ˌɒskə ˈwaɪld

Unit 13 /ɪ/ fill /iː/ feel

CAN YOU FEEL THE TANK, PLEASE?

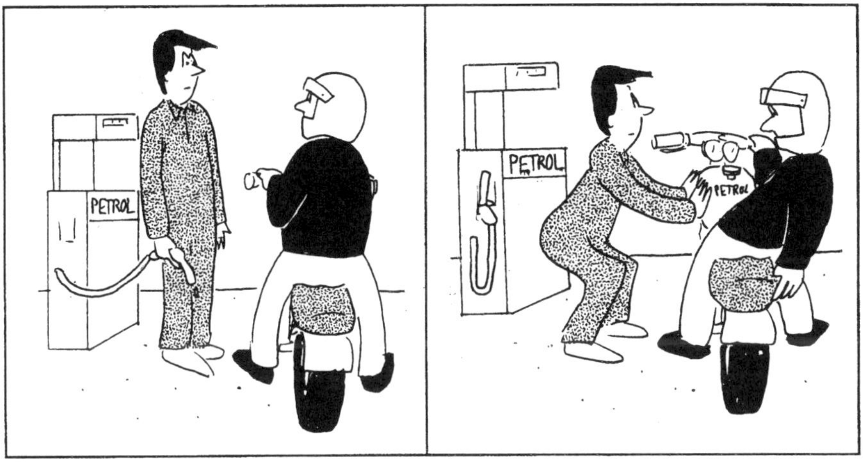

It is important not to confuse the two sounds /ɪ/ and /iː/ if you do not want to make embarrassing mistakes:

1. ***What are the answers to the following?***

A common farm animal from which we get wool?
The plural of foot?
A person who is in very good physical condition?
A large boat for carrying people across the sea?

2. Listening

2.1 ***Which is the odd one out?***

a. b. c. d.

2.2 ***Which word is being spoken? Underline the words you hear.***

dill	beat	pit	gene	team	fill	leap
deal	bit	peat	gin	Tim	feel	lip

3. Articulation of /ɪ/ and /iː/

/ɪ/ – The mouth should be relaxed.
Your tongue should lie at the
bottom of your mouth.
The sound is very short. Say *fit*

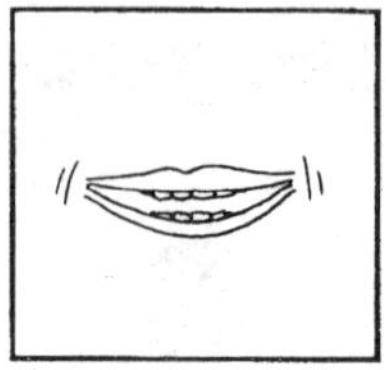

/ɪ/

/iː/ – The mouth is spread wider than for /ɪ/,
so the laugh lines become very prominent.
Your tongue should be raised
at the back, touching the soft palate.
The mouth is tense.
The sound is long. Say ***feet***

/iː/

4. Listen and Speak

4.1

/ɪ/:	bid	hill	pit	sin	hip	live	will
/iː/:	bead	heel	Pete	seen	heap	leave	we'll

4.2 Notice that before a voiced consonant /iː/ in particular is very much longer than before a voiceless consonant.

leaf	heat	leak	cease
leave	heed	league	sees

4.3

/ɪ/:	Sid	Liz	Philip	Lily	Linda	Billy the Kid	
/iː/:	Edith	Ian	Eve	Jean	Keith	Lee	Denise

/ɪ/	India	Brazil	England	Switzerland
/iː/:	Greenland	Egypt	Sweden	New Zealand

N.B.: The 'y' sound at the end of a word, as in *pretty, smelly*, is qualitatively the same as iː but considerably shorter. It is represented as i in all modern dictionaries and textbooks:

happy 'haepi̲ *totally* 'təʊtəli̲

Beware! A number of out-of-date books fail to use this notation.

4.4 Pronunciation of final '--ed'

There are three possible pronunciations for a final '-ed':

/d/ *pulled* /t/ *rushed* /ɪd/ *sorted*

(i) After voiceless consonants, '--ed' is pronounced as a /t/:

clipped	klɪpt	missed	mɪst	rushed	rʌʃt

(ii) After voiced consonants and vowels, including diphthongs, '--ed' is pronounced as a /d/:

pulled	pʊld	raised	reɪzd	wired	'waɪəd

(iii) After 't' or 'd', the '--ed' is always pronounced as an extra syllable /ɪd/:

exploded	ɪk'spləʊdɪd	heated	'hiːtɪd	voted	'vəʊtɪd

A few important adjectives also have the '-ed' pronounced as a syllable:

crooked	'krʊkɪd	ragged	'ræɡɪd
learned	'lɜːnɪd	wicked	'wɪkɪd
naked	'neɪkɪd	wretched	'retʃɪd

In most cases participles have the same pronunciation whether they are used as adjectives or verbs, as with *baked, cooked, watched*. However, some words have the '-ed' pronounced /ɪd/ when it is used adjectivally:

Say each of the following words twice, according to the endings shown in the two columns:

	past tense	**adjective**
learned	/d/	/ɪd/
blessed	/t/	/ɪd/
beloved	/d/	/ɪd/
aged	/d/	/ɪd/
crooked	/d/	/ɪd/

With some words the past tense form and the adjective are pronounced the same, but the -ed is pronounced /ɪd/ in the adverb form.

Say the following out loud:

past tense / adjective	**adverb**
advised	advisedly
alleged	allegedly
supposed	supposedly
marked	markedly
deserved	deservedly
unreserved	unreservedly

4.5 Tongue Twisters

She sells seashells on the seashore.
The shells that she sells are seashells, I'm sure.

Sixty-six sickly chicks, sixty-six sickly chicks.

5. Dialogue: Picnicking in a Field

Gareth: The peace in the country is unbeatable, isn't it?
Heather: Well, the city seems more real to me than these pretty scenes.
Gareth: But eating our picnic sitting under all these trees - it's idyllic.
Heather: What, with leaves in the sandwiches and beetles creeping over my feet?
Gareth: But I feel so free, breathing the sweet, clean air.
Heather: Gareth, why are you on your knees?
Gareth: Heather, you know how I feel about you. Will you marry me?
Heather: Oh please be reasonable and desist from this idiocy.
Gareth: But, Heather, my dearest beloved, be mine for eternity!
Heather: Really, Gareth. There is such a thing as being too sickly sweet in your sentiments.
Gareth: But will you consider me?
Heather: Possibly. After all, there are worse things than marriage: for example, illness and disease.
Gareth: I like a woman who's optimistic.

6. Stress shift in compound words

6.1 Listening

Listen to the words and the following phrases and notice what happens with the stress pattern.

The plane's automatic	-	the plane's on automatic pilot
She's old-fashioned	-	she wears old-fashioned clothes.

You will have noticed that the main stress in *automatic* and *old-fashioned* has changed. Generally speaking, the rhythm of English doesn't like strongly stressed syllables to follow each other and so, when such words with late stress are followed by strongly stressed words, the stress on the adjective

(i) shifts to an earlier syllable; and

(ii) becomes secondary.

The primary (main) stress shifts to the following noun:

good-looking	-	a good-looking boy
Chinese	-	a Chinese lantern
self-centred	-	a self-centred person

6.2 *Stress shifts*

Practise shifting the stress in the following compounds. In the phrases on the right, underline the new primary stress with two lines and the new secondary stress with one line. The first one has been done for you. Pronouce both columns out loud.

She's a student in her first semester.	-	She's a first-semester student.
There's a crisis in the Middle East.	-	the Middle East crisis
This suit is ready-made.	-	a ready-made suit
The watch is Japanese.	-	a Japanese watch
The number of pounds is nineteen.	-	nineteen pounds
The Union is European.	-	the European Union
This fact is well-known.	-	a well-known fact

7. Exercises

7.1 *Listen to the cassette and repeat the dialogue and listen and speak exercises until the /ɪ/ and /iː/ sounds are near-perfect.*

7.2 *Write out the following words in phonetic transcription. Check your answers with your dictionary.*

typically	indignity	Easter
believe	holiday	deceitful
pleasing	between	receive
demilitarise	religion	Christmas Eve

7.3 *What are the homophones?*

piːl: ________ ________

niːd: ________ ________ ________

ʤiːnz: ________ ________ ________

swiːt: ________ ________

piːt: ________ ________

fiːt: ________ ________

liːk: ________ ________

riːd ________ ________

7.4 ***Put the words below into the correct column according to the pronunciation of the '-ed'. Practise saying them aloud.***

watched	purchased	beloved (adj.)	ragged (adj.)
promised	croaked	arranged	pushed
dreaded	threatened	unashamedly	dragged
aged (adj.)	marred	lamented	learned (adj.)
jumped	allegedly	blessed (adj.)	crooked (adj.)

/d/	/t/	/ɪd/

7.5 ***If you pronounced the vowels underlined below wrongly, what might be understood?***

1. The dog bit the man.
2. The cars skid round the corner.
3. I've left my sheets on the bed.
4. I travelled by ship to Alaska.
5. World peace is worth working for.
6. I'm sorry to hurt your feelings.
7. We had beans on toast - lovely!
8. With a big leap he was able to cross the river.
9. I love this town. I never want to leave here.
10. Jean was always her favourite teacher.

7.6 ***Rewrite the following with the noun at the end. Underline the primary stress with two lines and the secondary stress with one line.***
Example:

arrangements made at the last minute = *last-minute arrangements*

1. The whole plan is half-baked. It's ____________________
2. This dictionary is monolingual. It's ____________________
3. Your carpenter is overworked. He's ____________________
4. The boy is bad-tempered. He is ____________________
5. Her memory is photographic. She has got____________________
6. The number of nails I bought is fifteen. I bought____________________
7. His views are old-fashioned. He's got ____________________
8. This man is good-looking. He's ____________________
9. The meal we had was first-class. It was____________________
10. He's a porter in a hotel. He's ____________________

7.7 ***Make phrases by connecting words from lines A, B and C. Underline the primary stress with two lines and the secondary stress with one line:***

e.g. anti-British placards

A	B	C
broad-	handed	wrestler
anti-	sleeved	compliment
well-	minded	professor
brand-	known	actor
absent-	headed	shoes
level-	term	***placards***
back-	shouldered	blouse
short-	new	prospects
long-	***British***	politician

7.8

SLEUTHMAN

Contracted forms: listen to this informal dialogue and fill in the missing words. Make sure you write down exactly what you hear. Then practise speaking the contractions.

Sleuthman:	Charlie? You in?
Charlie:	____________________ want?
Sleuthman:	I just ______________few words, that's all, Charlie.
Charlie:	What'm I supposed_____________done now?
Sleuthman:	There you are. I have reason to believe you were involved in the Worstmonster Bank raid last night.
Charlie:	Me? I_________________ done that! How many times_________________, Sleuthman. _______________ goin' straight fr' a year now.
Sleuthman:	Come off it, Charlie. Where were you last night? Have you got an alibi?
Charlie:	I was in the Black__________ with me mates. You can ask any____________.
Sleuthman:	And at around midnight?
Charlie:	I came straight 'ome. Ask_____ wife.
Sleuthman:	I have done. We caught her at Tesco's, spending £500 on the shopping.

7.9 ***Can you read these sayings and who said them? Do you agree with them?***

1. ˈpiːpl dɪmɑːnd ˈfriːdəm əv ˏspiːtʃ | tə ˌmeɪk ˈʌp fə ðə ˈfriːdəm əv ˏθɔːt | wɪtʃ ðeɪ əˎvɔɪd.

ˈkɪəkəgɑːd

2. haʊ ˈɪz ɪt ðət ˈlɪtl ˈtʃɪldrən ə səʊ ɪnˏtelɪdʒənt | əm ˈmen səʊ ˎstjuːpɪd? ɪt ˈmʌs bi edjuˎkeɪʃn ðət ˌdʌz ɪt.

ˌælɪgzɑːndə ˈdjuːmɑː

3. ˈnəʊ ˈmaen ˌfʊli ˈkeɪpəbl əv ɪz ˇəʊn ˌlæŋgwɪdʒ | ˈevə ˈmɑːstəz əˎnʌðə

ˌdʒɔːdʒ ˌbɜːnəd ˈʃɔː

KEY TO EXERCISES

KEY TO EXERCISES

Unit 1

5.3 Weak forms are underlined, strong forms are in **bold**.

1. He can come **too**. (Note that there is no weak form of *too*.)
2. She **must** have been mad **to** agree to **that**.
3. This poison isn't as effective as **that** one.
4. I'm not at all sure I know where **the** author comes **from**.
5. I would* have done **the** exam on the computer. (*strong ***or*** weak here)
6. She can **do** it **just** as well as he **can**.
7. What did you **do that for**?
8. **Do** I **have** to **do the** ironing?

5.5

J: *Oh, I see. But why do you work in such a run-down area?*
S: *Well, the nature of crime here means I have easy access to underground sources and I can keep up-to-date with the latest criminal methods.*
J: *Very interesting. What has been your most successful case so far?*
S: *Well, unfortunately the number of cases I deal with has been falling. Er, let me see. There's the case of industrial espionage that I solved.*
J: *Ah, the one at British Nuclear Fuels?*
S: *No, the one at Gertie's Ice Cream Parlour down the road. The Italian Mafia stole her recipe for Worcester Sauce flavoured ice cream.*
J: *Oh, you mean the case last year that we all read about in the tabloids?*
S: *No, no, you never read about the successful cases in the press!*
J: *I see. Well, there's no point in pressing you further. Thank you for your valuable time. I'm sure this area is safer due to your presence. Goodbye.*
S: *Goodbye. Mind you don't get mugged on the way out!*

Unit 2

3.6

1. buy, bye	6. awe, oar, ore	11. rows	16. dessert
2. rein, reign	7. isle, aisle	12. meter	17. source
3. sew, sow	8. weak	13. knew	18. plain
4. vain, vane	9. gnaw	14. witch	19. air
5. soars, saws	10. blew	15. pane	

3.7

1. milk and sugar	4. some bread and butter
2. half past eight	5. I'm from Japan.
3. five to nine	6. as quick as a flash

3.8 1. A: Doctor, Doctor, I feel like a pair of curtains.
B: Pull yourself together, man!

2. What's Dracula's favourite pudding?
I scream (ice cream)

3. What's the difference between a wet day and a lion with toothache?
One pours with rain and the other roars with pain.

4. Teacher: You're late. You should have been here at nine o'clock.
Boy: Why Miss, what happened?

5. Why did the boy throw the clock out of the window?
To see time fly.

Unit 3

1.1 a. 3 b. 2 c. 4 d. 1 e. 3

1.2

	1.	2.	3.	4.
a. thin	✓	✓		✓
b. thick	✓	✓	✓	
c. other	✓		✓	
d. worth		✓	✓	
e. breathe		✓	✓	✓
f. clothing		✓	✓	
g. there	✓		✓	

6.2 1. Too many cooks spoil the broth.
2. Don't throw the baby out with the bathwater.
3. Birds of a feather flock together.
4. God helps those that help themselves.
5. Set a thief to catch a thief.
6. A rolling stone gathers no moss.

6.3

Girls' names		Boys' names		Surnames	
/θ/	/ð/	/θ/	/ð/	/θ/	/ð/
Agatha	Heather	Arthur	-	Arthur	Booth
Anthea		Heath		Atherton	Fotherington
Edith		Keith		Heath	Heather
Elizabeth		Kenneth		Howarth	Sutherland
Ethel		Timothy		Keith	Weatherspoon
Judith				North	Worthington
Martha				Ruth	
Ruth				Thurber	
Thelma					

6.7

Sleuthman thumped hard on the front door of Fotherington Hall. Having run up the path, he was already out of breath and sprayed his mouth with the inhaler. "This damned asthma!", he cursed. Eventually, the chained door creaked open and the owner, Bruce Thackery, thrust his head through the gap.

"Ah, Inspector Sleuthman. Thanks for coming so promptly despite this filthy weather." Sleuthman followed him through the lengthy, gloomy corridor to the drawing room.

"What did the thief take?"
"Thieves, Inspector Sleuthman - there were three of them. They took three priceless paintings by Sutherland. There was nothing I could do - they threatened to slit my throat with a knife."

"They'll either have gone north to Heathrow Airport or south on the M3 to Portsmouth. We've set up road blocks. What about you?"
"Oh, I'll be O.K. I'm a bit shaken and I think they've broken my thumb."
"Sit down, breathe deeply and try to relax, Mr Thackery. I'm just going to look for some clues."

6.9

/ð/ Fotherington	/θ/ Sleuthman	
the (x10)	thumped	thieves
with	path	three (x3, incl.M3)
this	breath	nothing
weather	mouth	threatened
there	Thackery (x2)	throat
them	thrust	north
they (x4)	through (x2)	Heathrow
Sutherland	Thanks	south
They'll	filthy	Portsmouth
either	lengthy	think
breathe	thief	thumb

Word where the "th" is not normally pronounced at all: **asthma**

6.10 weather - Thursday   Thundery - three   whether - northerly
north - thicker   healthy - breathe

6.11 Sounds Maze - Below is a list of 36 words which you can certainly form. Can you find any more?

bath, breathe, breathing, broth, clothe, clothing, loth, loathe, loathing, nether, oath, rather, rhythm, thaw, thawing, thaws, the, them (weak form), then, those, though, thought, three, threes, throat, throb, throw, throws, throwing, weather, whether, whither, with, wither, wrath, wreath

Unit 4

1.1 a. 2   b. 4   c. 2   d. 1

1.2

	1.	2.	3.	4.
a.		✓	✓	
b.		✓	✓	
c.	✓			
d.			✓	✓
e.		✓		✓

4.1 The words with a dark 'l' are: well, mild, soul, sold

4.2 a. 3 b. 1 c. 1 d. 2

7.1 They are **all** stressed on the first syllable.

7.2 On the second syllable.

8.1

im**por**tant	be**came**	con**clude**	un**cer**tain
under**stand**	re**sponse**	il**le**gal	de**frost**

8.3
1. The strikers re**fuse** to go back to work without better conditions.
2. We always take our **ref**use to the dump at the weekend.
3. We don't fre**quent** the local theatre as much as we should do.
4. They are **fre**quent visitors to Dartmoor.

10.3 The first syllable is stressed unless the second syllable contains a long vowel or ends in two consonants. In this case, the second syllable is stressed.
If a word exists as a verb and a noun (or adjective), the verb has second-syllable stress and the noun first-syllable stress.

10.5

essay	**ac**cent	**sys**tem	**ac**tive	**pas**sive	**dec**ade	**chim**ney	de**sign**
margin	**ru**ler	**so**cial	ca**reer**	**meth**od	al**though**	hu**mane**	**en**gine
syntax	**en**ter	**e**qual	as**sist**	**en**vy	bal**loon**	per**suade**	ex**am**
justice	**hu**man	ho**tel**	**sat**ire	**san**dal	re**pair**	per**form**	**mo**tor

10.7

de~~bt~~	~~p~~sychology	~~k~~nife	ans~~wer~~	itiner~~ary~~	lam~~b~~
recei~~pt~~	~~p~~sychiatrist	w~~h~~ole	pref~~e~~rable	~~h~~our	wa~~l~~k
~~k~~nead	contemp~~orar~~y	su~~bt~~le	~~h~~onest	~~w~~rong	dou~~bt~~
libr~~ary~~	~~p~~neumonia	~~p~~salm	thum~~b~~	sa~~l~~mon	dum~~b~~
i~~r~~on	veg~~e~~table	a~~l~~mond	~~w~~reck	~~g~~nome	comf~~or~~table

10.8 1. **des**ert 2. ob**ject** 3. re**bel** 4. **in**sult 5. per**mit**
6. sub**ject**, **pro**gress 7. **produ**ce 8. per**fect** 9. **escort**

10.10 1. mountain 2. silk 3. doubt 4. Rome 5. silver
6. while 7. contempt 8. sweep 9. Absence 10. fire

10.11
(i) He's a nerve specialist who practises psychoanalysis.
(ii) This court's verdict was a miscarriage of justice.
(iii) Aren't you glad that this homework's almost completed?

Unit 5

1.1 a. 2 b. 1 c. 3 d. 1

1.2

	1.	2.	3.	4.
a. why	✓	✓	✓	
b. queen	✓			✓
c. wary		✓		✓
d. whale	✓	✓		
e. rowing			✓	✓

4.1 a. 4 b. 2 c. 3 d. 1

4.2

1. van	2. wheel	3. wet
4. vines	5. leaf	6. waive
7. life	8. save	9. first
10. wire	11. vile	12. fail

9.2

ac**tiv**ity	ar**tis**tic	au**thor**ity	**cat**like
Chi**nese**	**com**fortable	geo**graph**ic	**mu**sical
pro**duc**tion	refu**gee**	suc**cess**ful	usher**ette**

10.2

a**dorn**ment	al**lu**sion	ambi**gu**ity	as**sem**bly	as**sump**tion
at**trac**tive	**cir**culate	de**part**ment	edu**ca**tion	**foot**age
gene**ros**ity	**length**wise	**like**wise	ma**li**cious	mountai**neer**
mountainous	po**et**ic	**pref**erable	pro**duc**tive	re**duc**tion
re**quire**ment	**sen**sible	sur**viv**al	**sylph**like	**ten**dency

10.3

Sons and Lovers	*(D.H. Lawrence)*
The Power and the Glory	*(Graham Greene)*
Sense and Sensibility	*(Jane Austen)*
Crime and Punishment	*(Fyodor Dostoevsky)*
Romeo and Juliet	*(William Shakespeare)*
Dr. Jekyll and Mr. Hyde	*(Robert Louis Stevenson)*
The Old Man and the Sea	*(Ernest Hemingway)*
War and Peace	*(Leo Tolstoy)*
Dombey and Son	*(Charles Dickens)*
The Sound and the Fury	*(William Faulkner)*

10.8 (i) Most rock journalism is people who can't write interviewing people who can't talk for people who can't read.

Frank Zappa

(ii) Every decision you make is a mistake.

Edward Dahlberg

Unit 6

1.1 a. 3 b. 4 c. 1 d. 1

1.2

	1.	2.	3.	4.
a. man	✓	✓	✓	
b. sad		✓	✓	
c. can		✓		✓
d. track	✓	✓	✓	
e. mass	✓		✓	

4.1 a. 3 b. 1 c. 4 d. 3

8. ˌanni ˈversary ˌEuro ˈpean ˌdefi ˈnition
re ˌgene ˈration pro ˌnunci ˈation a ˈpostrophe

9.2
1. I thought you said **Mary** was coming tonight.
2. You **shouldn't** have gone to so much trouble.
3. Are **these** the keys you've been looking for?
4. Did Henry VIII want to get rid of **all** of his wives?

10.5
William Shakespeare
William Wordsworth
Charlotte Bronte
Thomas Hardy
George Orwell
Fay Weldon
George Eliot
John Fowles
Jane Austen
E. M. Forster
James Joyce
Virginia Woolf

10.6 Abbreviations

MD	Doctor of Medicine
PhD	Doctor of Philosophy
MA	Master of Arts
MSc	Master of Science
BA	Bachelor of Arts
BSc	Bachelor of Science
GCSE	General Certificate of Secondary Education

e.g.	exempli gratia (Latin = for example)
i.e.	id est (Latin = that is)
cf.	confere (Latin = compare)
viz.	videlicet (Latin = namely)
et. al.	et alia (Latin = and others)
ibid.	ibidem (Latin = in the same place)
N.B.	Nota Bene (Latin = note well)
PTO	please turn over
PM	Prime Minister
MP	Member of Parliament
MEP	Member of the European Parliament
UN	United Nations
NATO*	North Atlantic Treaty Organization
UNESCO*	United Nations Educational, Scientific and Cultural Organization
UNICEF*	United Nations International Children's Emergency Fund
lb.	pound = 454g
oz.	ounce = 28.35g
in.	inch = 2.54cm
m.p.h.	miles per hour

* These are common acronyms.

10.7 Idioms

1. It came out of the blue.
2. He's full of beans.
3. I've got pins and needles.
4. I haven't got a clue.
5. You've been ripped off.
6. I'd have been as sick as a parrot.
7. He can eat like a horse.
8. You'd have jumped out of your skin.

Unit 7

1.1 a. 4 b. 2 c. 2 d. 1

1.2 please lose lice hearse rays docks rips pads

8.2 ***Which is correct - /s/ or /z/ ?***

Plural forms:

road /z/	mat /s/	chair /z/	house /zɪz/	dock /s/	tube /z/
crash /ɪz/	theme /z/	eye /z/	rose /zɪz/	watch /ɪz/	lice!

Third person singulars:

look /s/	go /z/	run /z/	sit /s/	love /z/	help /s/
read /z/	fill /z/	say /sez/	choose /zɪz/	catch /ɪz/	lose /zɪz/

Possessive forms:

John /z/	Judith /s/	Edward /z/	Graham /z/	Joyce /sɪz/
Mary /ɪz/	Vince /sɪz/	James /zɪz/	Alice /sɪz/	Frank /s/

8.4 Sleuthman goes to the zoo

It was Thursday and Sleuthman decided to visit the zoo. He had heard that it was possible to learn about human behaviour by observing the animals. His first stop was the monkey house. "Gorillas resemble us most," he reasoned, but after a few minutes he saw nothing that would help with his work, so he moved on.
Where did he go next and why?
Write your answer here in phonetic script - fifty words please.

8.5 Recipe

For this recipe you need 200g of flour, half a pint of milk, one egg, a little water and a pinch of salt. First you mix the flour, water and milk, and then whisk in the egg. Keep whisking vigorously. Add a pinch of salt. Heat a little cooking oil in a frying pan, and when very hot, pour two tablespoonfuls of your mixture into it. Fry this on both sides until brown. What is it? What would you eat with it? (Pancakes)

8.7 Batman, spaceman, Superman, bogeyman, Sleuthman and strongman go in the left column, with an / æ / sound. All others have the schwa.

8.8 More abbreviations

BC	Before Christ
AD	Anno Domini
am	ante meridiem
pm	post meridiem
asap	as soon as possible

NASA*	National Aeronautics and Space Administration
CIA	Central Intelligence Agency
CID	Criminal Investigation Department
FBI	Federal Bureau of Investigation
RAF	Royal Air Force
HMS	Her Majesty's Service

BASIC	Beginner's All-purpose Symbolic Instruction Code (computer language)
DOS	Disc Operating System
http	hypertext transfer protocol
RAM	Random Access Memory
www	worldwide web
WYSIWYG	What You See Is What You Get
PC	Personal Computer
GP	General Practitioner
JP	Justice of the Peace
VIP	Very Important Person
RSVP	Répondez S'il-Vous Plaît (French = please reply)
UFO	Unidentified Flying Object
SOS	Save Our Souls
AIDS	Acquired Immune Deficiency Syndrome
BBC	British Broadcasting Corporation
ITV	Independent Television
RIP	Requiescat in Pace (Latin = Rest in Peace)
VAT	Value Added Tax
DIY	Do It Yourself
YUPPIE	Young Upwardly Mobile Professional Person
DINKY	Double Income, No Kids
NIMBY	Not In My Back Yard
MINT	Middle Income No Ties
LOMBARD	Lots Of Money But A Real Dickhead!

Unit 8

1.1 a. 2. should b. 2. foot c. 1. plume d. 1. swoon e. 1. prude
f. 2. wool g 1. soup h. 1. flute i. 2. good j. 1. mood

1.2 a. prune b. should c. dune d. route e. who'd

5.1 shirt earnings worm burnt serve colonel / kernel

9.3 Music soothes the savage breast.
The proof of the pudding is in the eating.
No news is good news.
Fortune favours the brave.
A bird in the hand is worth two in the bush.
First come, first served.
One good turn deserves another.

9.4 Crossword

Across:

1.	sofa	'səʊfə
3.	ugly	'ʌgli
6.	Noah	'nəʊə
7.	ouch	aʊʧ
8.	bow	baʊ
9.	dire	'daɪə
10.	Henry	'henri
11.	in	ɪn
13.	curse	kɜːs
14.	jaw	ʤɔː
15.	is	ɪz
16.	utter	'ʌtə
18.	drily	'draɪli

Down:

1.	sandwiches	'sændwɪʤɪz*
2.	flowers	'flaʊəz
3.	undress	ʌn'dres
4.	go	gəʊ
5.	laboratory	lə'bɒrətri
10.	hers	hɜːz
12.	gnaw	nɔː
13.	killed	kɪld
17.	sigh	saɪ

* *Sandwiches* has **six** possible transcriptions, of which this is probably the most frequent. See also the note on p.159, Unit 8.8.

9.5 Sleuthman couldn't keep up with the little rascal who had pickpocketed his wallet, but he did notice a slip of paper falling to the pavement. He snatched it up and memorised the telephone number on it. Through one of his unofficial liaisons, he managed to find out the address. He kept watch on the block of flats, hoping to catch sight of the boy. Eventually the boy staggered home, laden with bags and boxes. "Got you!" screamed Sleuthman.
"You've spent a lot, haven't you?"
"Well, you shouldn't keep your cheques and cheque card together!"

9.6

/uː/	/ʊ/
mood	crook
soup	hood
rue	wool
strewn	shook
crew	soot
cue	wood
prune	
fluke	

9.7	heard	/ɜː/	word	/ɜː/	yearn	/ɜː/
	heart	/ɑː/	fear	/ɪə/	tear	/eə/ or /ɪə/
	shirt	/ɜː/	wear	/eə/	ear	/ɪə/
	shears	/ɪə/	sword	/ɔː/	early	/ɜː/

9.8	fool	route / root	pearl	loose
	nurse	lose	suit	juice
	wood / would	curls	third	turf
	booth	murder	moose	surly

Unit 9

1.1 lab pig life had back rip prove clog

4.1 With /ən/ - Britain; all others: syllabic /n/. (But all could be said both ways.)

8.7 cups clocks white rope heat write back crap wet

8.8 **Joke Time**

1. What did the sea say to the beach? Nothing, it just waved.
2. What is black and white and read (red) all over? A newspaper.
3. Road safety notice outside a school:
   Drive carefully. Don't kill a child. Wait for a teacher.
4. Why does the ocean roar?
   Well, wouldn't you if you had crabs on your bottom?
5. Why can't you starve at the seaside?
   Because of the sand which is (sandwiches)* there.

* Of the six transcriptions of *sandwich*, the one in the joke is the only one that makes sense for the play on words *sand which* and *sandwich*. Note that *sand witch* is a homophone for this transcription. See also p.158, Unit 9.4.

8.10

/əʊ/	/ʌf/	/aʊ/	/ɔː/	/ə/	/ɒf/	/uː/
although dough though	rough enough tough	bough drought plough	ought bought fought brought sought nought	borough thorough	trough cough	through

Unit 10

2.1 pin tent curl bear dear gold

2.2 a. 4 b. 4 c. 2 d. 1

5.1 plaque great drain class brawn true

5.2 a. 3 b. 1 c. 4 d. 3

7.2

red dye	bright eyes	herb bread
top player	black ape	big goats

7.6

a. She was wearing a dee(p) purple dress.
b. They ha(d) dinner at nine o'clock.
c. We've got a fla(t) tyre, I'm afraid.
d. She gave him a bi(g) kiss.
e. What are my jo(b) prospects after the course?
f. I bought a large chest of drawers.
g. The nex(t) section's abou(t) ta(g) questions!
h. I waited for te(n) more minutes.
i. My teacher said I've got goo(d) pronunciation.

8.3

1. She is going to marry him, isn't she? ↘
2. You will come for dinner, won't you? ↘
3. You're not going to let him treat you like that, are you? ↗
4. They're not arriving today, are they? ↗
5. It's not true, is it? ↘
6. You still love me, don't you? ↗
7. You are taking your medicine, aren't you? ↘
8. You have paid, haven't you? ↘
9. John won't go, will he? ↘
10. You won't lose it, will you? ↘

10.2 The following combinations are easily imaginable. Others may be possible but contrived.

black	+	time - gap - pipe - dog - table - gate - cow - baby
bad	+	time - dog - cow - baby - job
great	+	time - gap - pipe - table - dog - gate - cow - baby - job (Both meanings of *great* are included.)
smart	+	dog - cow - baby
lead	+	pipe
good	+	time - dog - cow - baby - job
wide	+	gap - table - gate
big	+	time - gap - pipe - table - dog - gate - cow - baby - job
red	+	pipe - table - dog - gate - cow

10.3 blood - Great - Blood - drink

10.5 Correct sequence: a, g, e, i, d, j, f, h, c, b.

"I'm glad I've been going to the keep-fit class," muttered Sleuthman under his breath as he swiftly jumped over the four-foot railing. He flattened himself against the house wall and stayed in the shadow.
"I'm in luck," he whispered to himself as he found that the French window was unlocked. He let himself in. "Now, where would Doug Ugger hide papers?"
"They're all the same, these crooks, no respect for religion," he thought, as he detected the secret compartment in the statue of Jesus. Deftly he flicked open the little hinged door and took out the photos.
"Yup, these are the negatives. My client won't have to worry any more about being blackmailed."
"That was a good night's work," he chuckled as he stole quietly out of the garden.

10.6

1. Sadness only multiplies itself. Let us do our duty and be cheerful.

   Samuel Johnson

2. Clothes make the man. Naked people have little or no influence in society.

   Mark Twain

3. To be really medieval one should have no body. To be really modern one should have no soul. To be really Greek one should have no clothes.

   Oscar Wilde

Unit 11

1.1 chop joke ridge beseech

4.1.

leisure /ʒ/	issue /ʃ/	rouge /ʒ/	station /ʃ/	measure /ʒ/
television /ʒ/	decision /ʒ/	relation /ʃ/	usual /ʒ/	dishes /ʃ/

9.2

ˌWindsor 'Castle	ˌMadison Square 'Garden	ˌCovent 'Garden
ˌSpeakers' 'Corner	The ˌBrandenburg 'Gate	'Princes Street
ˌPall 'Mall	Vicˌtoria 'Station	The ˌRocky 'Mountains
Tra ˌfalgar 'Square	ˌWinchester Ca'thedral	'Wall Street
ˌSydney 'Harbour	ˌLong 'Island	'Downing Street
ˌPiccadilly 'Circus	ˌMexico 'City	The ˌTaj Ma'hal
The ˌGreat 'Lakes	ˌHorseguards Pa'rade	
The ˌEiffel 'Tower	ˌGolden Gate 'Bridge	

9.4 Sleuthman was ***choking*** when he said he didn't want the ***job***. It was all ***Chas's*** fault for patting him on the back just as he was about to swallow. For a moment he couldn't breathe, but then he lifted his ***chin***, swallowed, and felt much better. "Of course I want it," he said, secretly thinking what a ***chore*** it all sounded. Then he began shovelling pieces of meat into his mouth. His friend had just offered him the chance to ***shop*** an old enemy, Mr. ***Etch***, known for the carved initials he left at the scene of each successfully accomplished crime. "I'll begin right away."
Just as he was about to ask for the bill, Sleuthman remembered he only had small change in his jacket pocket. "Er, ***Chas***," he asked, "could I ***cadge*** a fiver off you? I'll pay you back tomorrow. Honest."

9.5 **Sounds puzzle**

1.	French fries	ˌfrenʧ 'fraɪz
2.	champagne	ʃaem'peɪn
3.	mushrooms	'mʌʃruːmz (*or* 'mʌʃrʊmz)
4.	porridge	'pɒrɪʤ
5.	chocolate	'ʧɒklət
6.	blancmange	blə'mɒn*d*ʒ
7.	gin	ʤɪn
8.	margarine	ˌmɑːʤə'riːn
9.	sherry	'ʃeri
10.	spinach	'spɪnɪʤ
11.	jam	ʤaem

Unit 12

1.1 bate lake raid taker way May

6.3

/eɪ/	/eə/	/aɪ/	/ɔɪ/	/əʊ/	/aʊ/	/ɪə/
beige rein slain convey snail veil prey	heir pear	tied sigh sleight rye	alloy toil	brooch mauve oats foe sew	rowdy	fear spear queer

6.4

travel agent's	**pep**per pot	semi-de**tached**	**book**shop
saltcellar	ham **sand**wich	**semi**circle	well-**ed**ucated
lemon juice	**black**bird	**rock**ing horse	outboard **mo**tor
front **door**	**bath**water	**wash**ing powder	paper **towel**
first **class**	**turn**ing point	pot-**bell**ied	**flow**erpot
well-**fed**	narrow-**mind**ed	**dish**washer	**liv**ing room
apple tree	apple **pie**	cherry **bran**dy	**cherr**y pip
plum **pud**ding	**plum** tree	tomato **soup**	to**ma**to plant
beef crisis	beef **stew**	**fish** knife	fish **fin**gers
cheesecake	**spring** water	**grape**fruit juice	milk **pud**ding
History teacher	central **heat**ing	mobile **phone**	**pon**ytail
dinner-jacket	**wat**er bottle	**fruit**cake	**clean**ing-lady

6.5

a wet **suit** (a suit that is wet)
a **wet**suit (a suit for divers)

an **Ital**ian teacher (She / he teaches Italian.)
an Italian **teach**er (He / she is Italian.)

a **driv**ing lesson (a lesson on how to drive)
a driving am**bi**tion (an ambition which strongly motivates s.o.)

a white **house** (a house which is white)
The **White** House (The U.S. President's home)

a **run**ning machine	(a machine for running on)
a running ma**chine**	(a machine that is in operation)
a travelling **sales**man	(a salesman who travels)
a **tra**velling bag	(a bag used for travelling)
a flying **sau**cer	(a UFO)
a **fly**ing club	(where you can learn to fly)
a rolling **stone**	(a stone which is rolling; (fig.) s.o. who travels a lot)
a **rol**ling pin	(a kitchen utensil whose function is to roll things flat)

6.6 ill-ad**vised**
landlady
hotel **por**ter
chatterbox
handwriting
cheese **sauce**
broken-**heart**ed
honeymoon
Prince **Charles**
Central **Sta**tion
ground **floor**
greenhouse
vacuum cleaner
blackcurrant **jam**
self-**sat**isfied

6.7 Pronunciation traps

dough	through	bird	bed	great
suite	debt	mother	bear	sword

6.9 Sayings

1. Education has produced a vast population able to read but unable to distinguish what is worth reading.

G.M. Trevelyan

2. Television is an invention that permits you to be entertained in your living room by people you wouldn't have in your home.

David Frost

3. All women become like their mothers. That is their tragedy. No man does. That's his.

Oscar Wilde

Unit 13

2.1 a. 3 b. 1 c. 3 d. 1

2.2 dill beat peat gene Tim fill leap

6.2
the Middle East crisis
a ready-made suit
a Japanese watch
nineteen pounds
the European Union
a well-known fact

7.3 **Homophones**

peal / peel
need / knead / kneed (past tense of verb 'to knee')
jeans / genes / Jean's
sweet / suite
Pete / peat
feat / feet
leak / leek
read / reed

7.4

/d/	/t/	/ɪd/
arranged threatened dragged marred	watched purchased promised croaked pushed jumped	beloved (adj.) ragged (adj.) dreaded unashamedly aged (adj.) lamented learned (adj.) allegedly blessed (adj.) crooked (adj.)

7.5

1. beat
2. skied
3. shits
4. sheep
5. piss
6. fillings
7. bins
8. lip
9. live
10. gin

7.6

1. a half-baked plan
2. a monolingual dictionary
3. an overworked carpenter
4. a bad-tempered boy
5. a photographic memory
6. fifteen stamps
7. old-fashioned views
8. a good-looking man
9. a first-class meal
10. a hotel porter

7.7 The following are some of the most obvious combinations but others are possible:

a broad-shouldered wrestler

a well-known actor

brand-new shoes

an absent-minded professor

a level-headed politician

a backhanded compliment

a long-sleeved blouse

short-term prospects

7.8

Sleuthman: Charlie. You in?
Charlie: What d'you want?
Sleuthman: I just wanna few words, that's all, Charlie.
Charlie: What'm I supposed to've done now?
Sleuthman: There you are. I have reason to believe you were involved in the Worstmonster Bank raid last night.
Charlie: Me? I wouldn't've done that! How many times've I got t'tell yer, Sleuthman, I've bin goin' straight fr' a year now.
Sleuthman: Come off it, Charlie. Where were you last night? Have you got an alibi?
Charlie: I was in the Black 'orse with me mates. You can ask any of 'em.
Sleuthman: And at around midnight?
Charlie: I came straight 'ome. Ask me wife.
Sleuthman: I have done. We caught her at Tesco's, spending £500 on the shopping.

7.9 (i) People demand freedom of speech to make up for the freedom of thought which they avoid.

Kierkegaard

(ii) How is it that little children are so intelligent and men so stupid? It must be education that does it.

Alexandre Dumas

(iii) No man fully capable of his own language ever masters another.

George Bernard Shaw

DIAGRAM OF MAIN SPEECH ORGANS

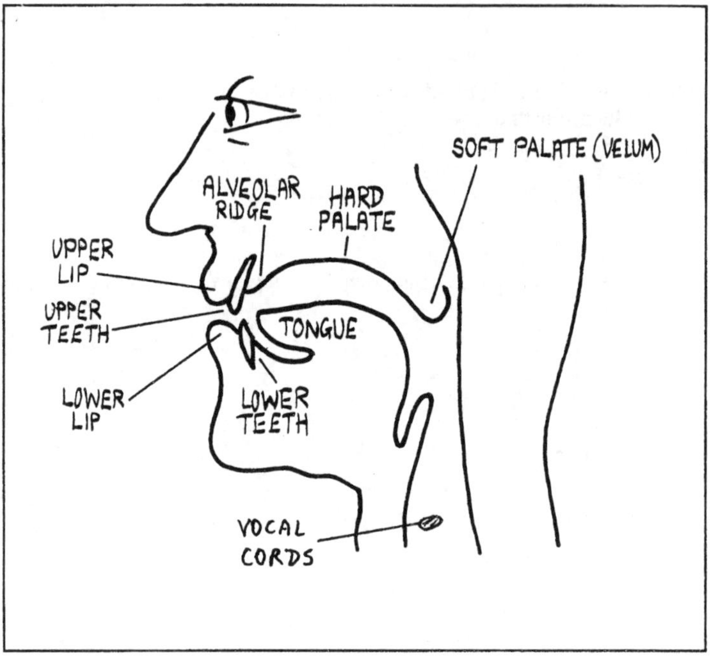

KEITH HOLLINGSWORTH and LAURA PARK are both Lecturers in English Language at the University of Dresden.